Celebrating Diversity:
Multicultural Education in Middle Level Schools

Celebrating Diversity:
Multicultural Education in Middle Level Schools

M. Lee Manning

NATIONAL MIDDLE SCHOOL ASSOCIATION

nmsa ®

NATIONAL MIDDLE SCHOOL ASSOCIATION

M. Lee Manning currently teaches language arts and middle level courses at Old Dominion University in Norfolk, Virginia. Dr. Manning, a former middle grades teacher, has co-authored two college level textbooks and numerous articles. He recently was appointed editor of the Association for Childhood Education International's newsletter, *Focus on Later Childhood/Early Adolescence.*

NMSA appreciates his willingness to share his scholarship and particularly his interest in integrating multicultural education into all facets of the middle school curriculum.

Photographs by Abe Bonowitz.

ISBN 1-56090-089-X

Contents

(Each chapter begins with a detailed outline of its contents)

Foreword

Now and always, the world has been one of physical and social diversity. Our nation, the United States of America, is a microcosm of the world, reflecting manifold evidence of physical, social, and human diversity. That diversity is the norm in this nation cannot be denied. Schools, therefore, as the cultural conduit of this nation, cannot be effective, whatever the extent of our nation's reform efforts, without the infusion of pluralism into their fundamental principles of cognitive, social, and affective schooling practices.

The current agenda for middle grades education even in pioneering documents such as *Turning Points: Preparing American Youth for the 21st Century* (1989), and *Caught in the Middle: Educational Reform for Young Adolescents in California Public Schools* (1987), is minimal in its list of, if at all attentive to, principles of multicultural education as essential elements of building effective middle schools. Little in our reform literature addresses cultural pluralism and multicultural infusion as critical to the transformation of education of young adolescents in this culturally diverse society.

There is no question that the agenda "welcomes into the mainstream of society those who might otherwise be left behind" (*Turning Points,* 1989, p. 3). But how "welcome" are "others"—those left behind—to a mainstream that "defines out," "falsifies," or "defames" their cultural background and experiences. Missing in our nation's middle grades reform agenda is the challenge to our schools to build a culture of respect for and understanding of the natural and social differences among the peoples of this nation through multicultural infusion throughout the total curriculum. Awareness of diversity among human beings and respect for the social pluralism that emanates from such diversity are necessary to "reserve a strong and vital America" (*Turning Points,* 1989, p. 15).

Turning Points further proclaims that "Educators agree that their mission includes teaching values for citizenship. These values include compassion, regard for human worth and dignity, respect for others' rights, tolerance and appreciation of human diversity, willingness to cooperate, and desire for social justice" (p. 45).

However powerful the wording and sincere the expectations, these "citizenship" goals cannot be achieved without an emphasis on pluralism and instructional practices imbued with the basic underlying principles of multicultural education. In our pluralistic society the learning environment for young adolescents must be reflective of that cultural diversity. The approach must be one of infusion, not merely additive of specific ethnic heroes, heroines, and holidays here and there. Incorporating diversity into developmentally appropriate instructional practices is essential in preparing American youth for the 21st century. It is this multicultural essentiality that Manning conveys in this monograph.

As Manning explains in considerable detail, several indicators point to a need for multicultural infusion at the middle level. Besides racism, crimes of hate, prejudice, and discrimination, of which middle level adolescents are well aware, they need to gain a better understanding of and tolerance for diverse populations. Moreover, young adolescents need to have their cultural experience recognized and appreciated. Early adolescence is a developmental period in which adolescents realize the "discrepancy between how people should be treated and how they actually are treated." And they are at an age whereby they can not only recognize racism, bias, prejudice (in others as well as themselves) but can also think critically about positive ways to deal with prejudice and can monitor evidence of it within themselves. What happens at this stage in their development can affect their attitudes and behaviors in high school and adulthood. This is why anything less that a comprehensive infusion of multicultural education across the total school curricula will not suffice as reformed middle level education.

This monograph is not merely a text of theories and propositions but a practical guide to multicultural instruction. For example, the comprehensive chapter that annotates appropriate curricular resources is very useful. However, most valuable to teachers and educational leaders are suggestions for improving their selection and development of materials, improving their design and implementation of multicultural curricula, and applying alternative assessment practices that foster equal access to learning for all young adolescents. Not only does he explain why multicultural education at the middle level is important but also how teachers and educational leaders might design multicultural curricula. Practical suggestions constitute the core of this monograph.

The principal message Manning conveys is that only a "full scale" effort will have optimal effects. That is, multicultural educational programs must be "integrated in all areas of the school day—curricula experiences, instructional materials, and all the essential middle level school components such as advisories and exploratories." Anything less than a full scale effort will not suffice as multicultural education and, therefore, will not even begin to realize the lofty goals and ideals of the middle school movement.

Advocates of multicultural education who have grown weary of so-called multicultural education instructional guides that emphasize only the toils, snares, and outrageous conditions of people of color in this nation will find instructional suggestions in this monograph much more inspiring, perhaps refreshing. Without giving illusions of progress in racial and gender relations in this country, Manning attempts to balance his curricular examples with reflections of positive along with negative conditions and noteworthy accomplishments of culturally diverse people in this nation. Both realities are emphasized.

A particular strength of this monograph is its enrichment of the fundamental reform agenda by calling for the convergence of the middle school reform movement and the multicultural education movement. Although both movements strongly advocate educational equity for all students and total school reform, the multicultural education movement, more strongly than the middle grades reform agenda, emphasizes a comprehensive reform agenda that seeks to ensure that multiculturalism permeate all facets of middle level learners' education.

In the midst of transforming middle level education, *Celebrating Diversity: Multicultural Education in Middle Level Schools,* calls to our attention a missing link in the reform movement. As we re-examine our paradigms and practices, we must not overlook the diversity that inspires the basic principles of democracy in this society. Since schools reflect a nation's culture, our middle school curriculum and social practices must reflect a total curriculum imbued with diversity and pluralism. We "celebrate diversity" only through total curriculum transformation.

—Betty McEady-Gillead
Publications Committee
NMSA

Preface

The middle school movement, with considerable support from the National Middle School Association, its forty-nine affiliates, and thousands of dedicated middle level school educators, has made real progress in improving the educational experiences of young adolescents. Challenges such as designing a developmentally appropriate curriculum for 10-15 year olds, implementing teacher advisory and exploratory programs, and providing other appropriate educational experiences are being met with clear success. Our nation's steadily increasing cultural diversity poses still another challenge for middle level educators. Instituting an effective multicultural education program will result in rich dividends for all young adolescents.

Perceptive middle level educators have recognized the need for comprehensive multicultural education programs. The United States is experiencing tremendous growth in the number and size of culturally diverse populations. Native Americans, while not increasing at rapid rates, still inhabit the country they once considered their common heritage. African Americans' relatively young population and high birth rates mean their population will likely exceed 34 million by the year 2000. Influxes of Asians continue to add to their increasing number. Hispanic Americans have among the highest population increases and, if predictions are realized, will outnumber African Americans and people of any other single minority cultural background by the second decade of the 21st century. Last, many European, African, and Australian immigrants add to our nation's diversity.

Several indicators point to a need for comprehensive and effective multicultural education programs. First, as previously stated, our nation continues to be characterized and enriched by an increasingly diverse population. Second, racism, crimes of hate, prejudice, and discrimination continue to plague the United States. Young people must recognize the ill effects of failing to accept others and their differences. Third, majority culture learners need to gain a better understanding of culturally diverse populations and the challenges these groups face in a majority culture society. Fourth, culturally diverse young adolescents need to see their cultural differences and backgrounds as recognized and appreciated.

Research and writing on multicultural education, while relatively new, have progressed to a point where significant programs can be implemented. The work of several scholars in the field, several excellent books, many journal articles, and Canada's commitment to multiculturalism suggest the late 1990s and the 21st century are times for genuine efforts toward achieving positive multiculturalism.

While all levels of schooling have a responsibility to teach multiculturalism, the middle level school has an even greater responsibility. Young adolescents are in a developmental period that allows them to realize the discrepancy between how people should be treated and how they actually are treated. Likewise, young adolescents are at an age where they can thoughtfully consider racism, bias, prejudice, and discrimination. Middle level educators teach young adolescents at a time when their understanding of others and their differences are being formed, with the resulting attitudes likely to last a lifetime.

Celebrating Diversity: Multicultural Education in Middle Level Schools proposes that young adolescents need comprehensive multicultural education programs that are integrated in all areas of the school day—curricular experiences, instructional materials, and all the essential middle level school components such as advisories and exploratories. The main premise of this monograph is that anything less than a full-scale effort will not suffice.

Chapter 1 looks at our nation's increasing cultural diversity and the hurdles culturally diverse learners face. Chapter 2 explores the concept of multicultural education and such societal ills as racism, prejudice, and discrimination. Chapter 3 looks at essential middle school concepts and program elements such as teacher advisory programs, communities of learning, and exploratory programs and explains how these middle school areas can reflect multiculturalism. Continuing the current middle school emphasis on improving curricular experiences for young adolescents, Chapter 4 focuses on curriculum and proposes all curriculum designs and efforts must include multiculturalism —neither as simply a narrow thread in an integrated unit nor as a "special" week or day — but as a full-scale effort. Since young adolescents' success in mastering the curriculum depends to a significant extent on their competence in English, a section in Chapter 4 examines appropriate teaching strategies for linguistically different learners.

Providing much more than simply a bibliography, Chapter 5 lists resources that teachers can consult and secure. Readers are given addresses of professional associations, organizations promoting the welfare of specific cultural groups, and several state departments of education that have developed multicultural materials.

Multicultural education programs will surely become significant aspects in middle level schools, for middle level educators have successfully met other challenges and will rally behind the effort to promote multiculturalism. Young adolescents' developmental needs and academic welfare have always been at the forefront of the movement, and understanding multiculturalism as a contemporary need of young adolescents will also receive major attention.

The middle school movement has already had a powerful and positive impact on the education of young adolescents. The challenge for the few remaining years of the 1990s and the upcoming 21st century will be for educators to continue to address the unique developmental needs of culturally diverse learners and to provide teaching-learning experiences which genuinely reflect and celebrate multiculturalism.

Middle level schools can become even more significant in the lives of young adolescents and can become a model for other schools to emulate when teachers deal with cultural diversity in such a way that our curriculum is enriched, there is an ongoing demonstration of respect for all people regardless of differences and when all forms of ill treatment are attacked. This monograph urges middle level educators to accept the challenge of making multiculturalism an essential element in the middle school concept.

August 1994

M. Lee Manning
Old Dominion University

1

Our Increasingly Multicultural Society

Cultural differences are strengths that enrich our democratic society.

CHAPTER OUTLINE

Our Increasingly Multicultural Society   1

The increasingly diverse population of the United States and the importance of young adolescents forming positive perceptions toward others challenge middle level educators to plan and implement effective multicultural education programs. Young adolescents' psychosocial and cognitive development leads to the formation of personal attitudes and perspectives toward cultural, ethnic, gender, social class, and individual differences among people. Prerequisite to launching an effective multicultural education program is gaining an understanding of diversity and its challenges by all faculty and staff. Based firmly on the belief that differences among people enrich both the United States and its schools, this chapter examines the cultural diversity of the nation and challenges middle level educators to provide responsive multicultural education programs and experiences.

Cultural Diversity: Past and Present

The United States has opened its doors to people of diverse cultural, ethnic, and racial origins for many years. Some people entered the country with hopes of achieving the American dream, while others immigrated as a means of getting away from oppressive conditions. Others came against their will and were expected to become culturally similar to the Anglo-American population. Still others, who first inhabited the land on which the United States now exists, were expected to adopt the "white man's" ways.

Our society continues to grow more culturally diverse. Current population numbers include 30 million African Americans, 1.5 Native Americans, 7.3 million Asian Americans; 22.4 million Hispanic Americans. Projections suggest 35 million African Americans and 5.5 million 5-17 year old Hispanic Americans by 1995 (U.S. Bureau of the Census, 1991a). Also, there are another 112.4 million people from the various European countries (U.S. Bureau of the Census, 1992). Specific cultural groups will be described in a later section.

Historical perspectives toward cultural diversity

Historically, many in the U.S. believed cultural differences were "deficits" to be remediated. Popular notions existed which even considered culturally diverse people intellectually inferior and less able to learn. Likewise, they were socially maladjusted and, therefore, a nuisance or a threat to society. The nation held schools and other social institutions responsible for eliminating cultural traditions and backgrounds. Through activities commonly associated with daily living and working together, these people were expected to adopt "American" customs and values, and through a "melting pot" actually became assimilated into mainstream "Americans." For a number of reasons, however, many culturally diverse people rejected the melting pot ideology. These differing ethnic groups sought to retain their unique cultural identity and heritage and wanted their cultural differences recognized and valued.

Glazer and Moynihan (1970) in their book, *Beyond the Melting Pot,* proposed that the melting pot metaphor used to describe the cultural composition of the United States did not, in reality, ever provide an accurate description. To strengthen their point, Glazer and Moynihan explained how Jews, Italians, and the Irish of New York City chose to retain their old world heritages. Similarly, other groups also failed (or elected not to try) to forsake cherished cultural characteristics in order to become "Americanized." Asians and Hispanics often hesitated to give up ethnic customs and traditions in favor of "middle-class American habits" which appeared contrary to beliefs taught early in life. African Americans fought to overcome cultural dominance and discrimination, and, through efforts such as the Civil Rights movement, sought to understand and maintain their cultural heritage. This need to recognize and respect individual differences and similarities within cultures becomes clear when one considers the geographical, generational, and social class differences among the Native American, African, Asian, Hispanic, and European cultures.

Contemporary perspectives toward cultural diversity

While some cultural assimilation undoubtedly occurred as culturally diverse people adopted Anglo customs and standards, generally speaking, the melting pot idea began to adjust to a perspective of the U.S. society being a "salad bowl" wherein each group reflected its unique identity and its American experience (McCormick, 1984). The salad bowl concept, whereby all people live together yet hold onto distinctive cultural backgrounds, holds more realistic possibilities and humane expectations for the U.S. to adopt. Whether arriving from Southeast Asia, one of the many Spanish-speaking countries, or one of the many other areas from which immigrants have come, people should not be expected to forsake their cultural heritages and traditions. Admittedly, some degree of assimilation may be necessary for successful participation in the U.S. economy, i.e., English skills which are appropriate for coping with everyday life and the job skills necessary to secure employment. Even with this degree of assimilation, however, culturally different people can still be allowed or, indeed, encouraged to hold onto cherished and time-honored cultural customs and traditions. While the melting pot ideology appeared to perceive differences as entities to be eradicated, the more enlightened salad bowl ideology views differences as being personal characteristics which contribute to and enrich our democratic society.

Rather than provoking anger or causing fear, cultural differences in values, customs, and traditions should be celebrated as a means of enriching the United States. Likewise, culturally diverse learners deserve to be viewed objectively without stereotyping and discrimination. People who perceive differences as enriching may not eliminate racism and acts of violence; however, celebrating differences continues to be an important step, especially if efforts focus upon those learners who will lead the nation during the 21st century. Considering differences to be strengths, however, is only a beginning. Significant change will take more comprehensive and deliberate efforts.

Middle level schools' responsibilities during the 1990s and the 21st century

The cultural diversity that characterizes the American nation extends into the schools where children of all cultures learn, interact, and share all curricular experiences. Since young adolescents are now able to perceive and be sensitive to differences among people, multicultural education is an imperative in contemporary middle level schools. Psychosocial and cognitive changes allow young adolescents to perceive cultural differences as assets rather than deficits. Early adolescence is a most crucial stage for the formation of positive attitudes toward cultural differences.

Middle level schools face several significant challenges in the next few decades, especially when one considers the importance of young adolescents forming attitudes compatible with the ideals of a democratic society. Middle level schools can help culturally diverse people who want to hold onto valued customs and beliefs and, simultaneously, live in a land where acceptance and equality prevail. They can take an active stance against racism, sexism, classism, bigotry, and crimes of hate. Middle level schools have a rare opportunity to contribute to young adolescents' understanding democratic values and having dreams of a positive pluralistic society.

Middle level educators' success in providing educational experiences reflecting multiculturalism will depend upon the extent of their agenda and their commitment to support the effort. The benefits to young adolescents, their schools, community, and the nation itself will justify the toil.

The Culturally Different

This section presents current and projected population numbers of selected culturally diverse groups, provides geographical information when available, and offers other demographic information. The U.S. Census Bureau does not report the same information on all cultural groups, so population projections available for one cultural group may not be available for another group.

Native Americans

Comparatively speaking, Native Americans have small population numbers and the smallest increases in recent decades. Native Americans, however, still warrant consideration because they represent significant numbers in several states and because Native American children experience many problems which schools can address (Sanders, 1987). The total Native American population is approximately 1.5 million or one-half percent of the total U.S. population. Ten to fourteen year olds account for approximately 188,000 or 12.5% of the total Native American population (U.S. Bureau of the Census, 1992). Projections show growth of the American Indian population, reaching 4.6 million by 2050 (U.S. Bureau of the Census, 1990, September.). Table 1-1 shows the ten largest Native American tribes.

TABLE 1-1: Ten Largest Native American Tribes

Tribe	Numbers	
Cherokee	308,000	
Navajo	219,000	
Chippewa	104,000	
Sioux	103,000	
Choctaw	82,000	
Pueblo	53,000	Compiled from: U.S. Bureau of the Census, (1990, September). *We the ... First Americans.* C 3.2: AM 3/19. Washington, DC: Author, p. 2.
Apache	50,000	
Iroquois	9,000	
Lumbee	48,000	
Creek	44,000	

In 1990, 437,000 Native Americans lived on reservations and associated trust lands. Of the Native Americans living on the 314 reservations, 388,000 lived on the 78 reservations with 1,000 or more Native Americans. The Navajo Reservation and Trust Lands in Arizona, New Mexico, and Utah comprise the largest of the reservations (U.S. Bureau of the Census, 1991b). States with the largest number of

American Indians, Eskimos, and Aluets in 1990 included (in thousands) Oklahoma - 252; California -242, Arizona -204; New Mexico - 134; Alaska -86; Washington - 81; North Carolina - 80; Texas - 66; New York - 63; and Michigan - 56 (U.S. Bureau of the Census, 1990, September).

African Americans

The African American population increased to nearly 30 million in 1990. With a 13.2% increase since 1980, their growth rate was one-third higher than the national growth rate (U.S. Bureau of the Census, 1991b). In fact, the African American population has been growing faster than the total population for a number of years, i.e., their population increased from 11.8% in 1980 to 12.2% in 1987 (Black population is growing..., 1988). Likewise, the African American population during the next few decades will probably outpace the Anglo population because of the relatively young age of the African American population (U.S. Bureau of the Census, 1986). Ten to fourteen year olds account for 2.6 million (U.S. Bureau of the Census, 1992) with project numbers of 7.9 million of 5 to 17 year olds by the year 2,000 (U.S. Bureau of the Census, 1991a). Table 1-2 provides population numbers for all African Americans and for 10-14 year olds.

TABLE 1-2: African-American Population by Sex and Age: 1992		
	Population Numbers All Ages	Population Numbers 10-14 Year Olds
Female	15,816,000	1,287,000
Male	14,170,000	1,314,000
Compiled from: U.S. Bureau of the Census. (1992). *Statistical abstracts of the United States* (112th ed.). Washington, DC: Author, p. 18.		

The African American population in 1990 exceeded one million in sixteen states and exceeded two million in three states—New York, California, and Texas. Other states with significant African American populations (one million or more) include Florida, Georgia, Illinois, North Carolina, Louisiana, Michigan, and Maryland (U.S. Bureau of the Census, 1993a, September).

Table 1-3 shows the ten cities with the largest African American populations in 1990:

TABLE 1-3: Ten Largest Cities With African American Populations

City	Population
New York	2,103,000
Chicago	1,088,000
Detroit	778,000
Philadelphia	632,000
Los Angeles	488,000
Houston	458,000
Baltimore	436,000
Washington, DC	400,000
Memphis	335,000
New Orleans	308,000

Compiled from: U.S. Bureau of the Census, (1993a, September). *We the American... Blacks.* C 3.2: AM 3/14 Washington, DC: Author, p. 4.

Asian Americans and Pacific Islanders

Boosted by high levels of immigration, the Asian and Pacific Islander population more than doubled from 3.5 million in 1980 to 7.3 million in 1990 (U.S. Bureau of the Census, 1991b). For the last two decades, the number of Asians and Pacific Islanders in the United States has doubled, from 1.5 million in 1970 to 3.7 million in 1980 to 7.3 million in 1990 (U.S. Bureau of the Census, 1993b. September). The ten states with the largest Asian and Pacific Islander population in 1990 included California, New York, Hawaii, Texas, Illinois, New Jersey, Washington, Virginia, Florida, and Massachusetts. Ten to fourteen year olds totaled 552,000 in 1990 or 7.5% of the total Asian American population (U.S. Bureau of the Census, 1992).

Tremendous differences exist among Asian and Pacific Islander people. It is highly inappropriate to assume they are a single entity. Table 1-4 shows total population numbers and numbers of 10-14 year olds from various Asian groups.

Asian Americans can also include refugees from Southeast Asia and often include Blue, White, and Striped Hmong; Chinese, Krom, and Mi Khmer Cambodians; Chinese Mien, Thai Dam, and Khmer Laotians; and Lowlander and Highlander Vietnamese. Each Asian group has its own history and culture as well as many stratifications within each group (Kitano, 1989).

Table 1-4: Asian Populations in the United States

Cultural Group	Total Population Numbers	Population Numbers of 10-14 Year Olds
Asian or Pacific-Islander	7,226,986	551,483
Asian	6,876,394	516,781
Chinese	1,574,918	100,418
Taiwanese	73,778	6,909
Filipino	1,419,711	110,178
Japanese	886,160	40,128
Asian Indian	786,694	65,878
Korean	797,304	63,006
Vietnamese	593,213	53,952
Cambodian	149,047	14,923
Hmong	94,439	11,245
Laotian	147,375	18,517
Thai	91,360	7,107
Indonesian	30,085	1,462
Pakistani	81,691	5,940
Pacific-Islander	350,592	34,702
Polynesian	283,885	28,453
Hawaiian	205,501	19,949
Samoan	57,679	6,386
Tongan	16,707	1,877
Micronesian	54,970	5,324
Guamanian	47,754	4,637
Melanesian	7,218	567

Adapted from: U.S. Bureau of the Census. (1990a). *Asians and Pacific Islanders in the United States.* C 3.223.10: 1990 CP-3-5. Washington, DC: Author, pp. 1-35.

Table 1-5 provides a percentage breakdown for selected Asian populations living in the United States in 1990.

Approximately 66 percent of Asians in 1990 lived in just five states: California, New York, Hawaii, Texas, and Illinois. Other states with the greatest Asian populations included Washington, Florida, Virginia, Michigan, Pennsylvania, New Jersey, Maryland, Delaware, Connecticut, and Massachusetts (U.S. Bureau of the Census. 1993b, September).

The 1990 census counted 365,024 Pacific Islanders, a 41 percent increase over the 1980 count of 259,566. Specific groups include Polynesian, Micronesian, and

Table 1-5: Asian Population, Selected Groups: 1990

Chinese	23.8	
Filipino	20.4	
Japanese	12.3	
Asian Indian	11.8	
Korean	11.6	
Vietnamese	8.9	
Laotian	2..2	
Cambodian	2.1	
Thai	1.3	
Hmong	1.3	
Other Asian	4.4	
Burmese	0.1	Compiled from: U.S. Bureau
Sri Lankin	0.2	of the Census. (1993b.
Bangladeshi	0.2	September). *We, the*
Malayan	0.2	*American ...Asians.* C 3.2: AM
Indonesian	0.4	3/13. Washington, DC:
Pakistani	1.2	Author.
All other Asian	2.1	

Melanesian backgrounds. The Polynesian groups is the largest and includes Hawaiians, Samoans, Tongans, and Tahitians. The Micronesian group is primarily Guamanian and also includes other Mariana Islanders, Marshall Islanders, Palauans, and several other groups. The Melanesian group contains mostly the Fijian populations (U.S. Bureau of the Census. 1993c, September). Table 1-6 examines percentages of selected Pacific Islander populations living in the United States in 1990.

Approximately 75 percent of Pacific Islanders in 1990 lived in just two states: California and Hawaii. These two states have more than 100,000 Pacific Islanders. Washington was the only other state with 15,000 or more Pacific Islanders (U.S. Bureau of the Census, 1993c, September).

Hispanic Americans

As with Asian Americans, providing Hispanic American population numbers proves difficult because of the tremendous range of Spanish speaking countries and people. The Hispanic population from 1980 to 1990 increased from 14.6 million to 22.4 million. This 53 percent increase resulted from a high birth rate as well as high levels of immigration. Selected specific Hispanic populations that the U.S. Bureau of the Census selected for detailed examination revealed the following

Table 1-6: Distribution of the Pacific Islander Population: 1990

	Percent
Hawaiian	57.8
Samoan	17.2
Guamanian	13.5
Tongan	4.8
Fijian	1.9
Palauan	0.4
Northern Mariana Islander	0.3
Tahitian	0.3
All other Pacific Islanders	3.8

Compiled from: U.S. Bureau of the Census. (1993c, September). *We, the American ...Pacific Islanders.* C 3.2: AM 3/15. Washington, DC: Author, p.1.

increases: Mexican - 54.4%; Puerto Rican - 35.4%; and Cuban - 30.0% U.S. Bureau of the Census. (1993d, November).

Ten to fourteen year olds in 1990 totaled 2,002,000 (U.S. Bureau of the Census, 1992); however, projections suggest Hispanic 5-17 year olds will reach 6,207,000 by the year 2000, a 28.6% increase (U.S. Bureau of the Census, 1991a). If predictions become reality, Hispanics will outnumber African Americans and people of any other single minority background. In fact, Hispanics currently outnumber African American in cities such as New York, Los Angeles, San Diego, Phoenix, San Francisco, and Denver (U.S. Bureau of the Census, 1988). Table 1-7 provides population numbers of Hispanic groups.

Table 1-8 offers a percentage breakdown of the Hispanic population living in the United States in 1990.

Table 1-9 shows the states with significant Hispanic populations.

European, African, Australia, and other cultural groups

Other cultural groups also inhabit the United States, adding to its diversity. Table 1-10 provides population numbers of European, African, Australian, and other cultural groups.

Table 1-7: Hispanic Populations in the United States

Cultural Group	Population Numbers	Population Numbers of 10-14 Year olds
Mexican	13,393,208	1,303,808
Puerto Rican	2,651,815	260,660
Cuban	1,053,197	49,512
Dominican Republic	520,151	42,683
Central Ameican	1,323,830	101,067
Costa Rican	57,223	4,174
Guatemalan	268,779	19,173
Honduran	131,066	10,220
Nicaraguan	202,658	17,980
Panamanian	92,013	6,086
Salvadoran	565,081	42,922
South American	1,035,602	68,698
Argentinean	100,921	5,675
Bolivian	38,073	2,849
Chilean	68,799	4,286
Colombian	378,726	25,928
Ecuadorian	191,198	12,573
Paraguayan	6,662	328
Peruvian	175,035	12,014
Uruguayan	21,996	1,336
Venezuelan	47,997	3,295
Spaniard	519,136	35,977
Spanish	444,896	35,768
Spanish American	93,320	9,477

Compiled from: U.S. Bureau of the Census. (1990b). *Persons of Hispanic Origin in the United States*. C 3.223.10: 1990 CP-3-3. Washington, DC: Author, pp. 1-38.

Table 1-8: Hispanic Population by Type of Origin: 1990

Percentages

Mexican		61.2
Puerto Rican		12.1
Cuban		4.8
Dominican		2.4
Other Hispanic		3.9
Spaniard		4.4
Central American		6.0
Costa Rican	4.3	
Panamanian	7.0	
Honduran	9.9	
Nicaraguan	15.3	
Guatemalan	20.3	
Salvadorian	42.7	
Other Central American	2.1	
South American		4.7
Chilean	6.6	
Argentinean	9.7	
Peruvian	16.9	
Ecuadorian	18.5	
Colombian	36.6	
Other South American	11.7	

Compiled from: U. S. Bureau of the Census. (1993d, November). *We the American... Hispanics.* C 3.2: AM 3/18/993-2. Washington, DC: Author, p. 4.

Table 1-9: Hispanic Population for Selected States: 1990

State	Percentage Distribution of Hispanic Population
California	34.4
Texas	19.4
New York	9.9
Florida	7.0
Illinois	4.0
New Jersey	3.3
Arizona	3.1
New Mexico	2.6
Colorado	1.9
Massachusetts	1.3
All other states	13.0

Compiled from: U. S. Bureau of the Census. (1993d, November). *We the American... Hispanics.* C 3.2: AM 3/18/993-2. Washington, DC: Author, p. 3.

Table 1-10: Other Selected Cultural Groups by Country of Birth: 1990

Country of Birth	Population	
Europe		112.4
Czechoslovakia	1.4	
France	2.8	
Germany	7.5	
Greece	2.7	
Hungary	1.7	
Ireland	10.3	
Italy	3.3	
Netherlands	1.4	
Poland	20.5	
Portugal	4.0	
Romania	4.6	
Soviet Union	25.5	
Spain	1.9	
Sweden	1.2	
Switzerland	0.8	
United Kingdom	15.9	
Yugoslavia	2.8	
Africa		35.9
Egypt	4.1	
Nigeria	8.8	
South Africa	2.0	
Australia		1.8
New Zealand and other countries		4.5

Compiled from: U.S. Bureau of the Census. (1992). *Statistical abstracts of the United States* (112th ed.). Washington, DC: Author, p. 11.

Understanding Diversity

Perceptive middle level educators have long recognized the tremendous developmental differences in 10-14 year olds. More recently, emphasis has been placed on recognizing other equally important differences: culture, ethnicity, gender, social class, and with some learners, generational differences. Educational experiences reflecting an understanding of diversity provide for differences among learners rather than catering to the predominant cultural group and directing teaching-learning experiences toward one gender. Understanding diversity and committing to plan educational experiences reflecting diversity will be a prime responsibility of the middle level school as diverse learners continue to increase and since young adolescents are forming self-concepts, cultural identities, and lifelong attitudes toward others.

Culture

An understanding of culture and its effects on learning and behavior is prerequisite to effective multicultural education programs in middle schools. Culture has been defined in several ways:

- the way people use, interpret, and perceive values and symbols which distinguish one people from another (Banks, 1992)

- institutions, language, values, religion, ideals, habits of thinking, artistic expressions, and patterns of social and interpersonal relationships (Lum, 1986)

- elements of people's history, traditions, values, and social organization that become meaningful to participants in an encounter (Green, 1982)

While an understanding of culture is crucial in multicultural settings, understanding how individuals' culture affects their learning and behavior may be more important. Because of culture, people have differing values and perspectives of the world, and therefore, behave and act differently toward one another because of their values and world perspectives (Crawford, 1993). Peoples' behavior reflects the logical beliefs of their culture which actually serves as their frame of reference (Smith & Otero, 1985).

Understanding culture is, then, important to educators of 10-14 year olds. Expecting all cultural groups to act like middle-class Anglo American learners can be a dangerous assumption on which to build educational experiences. Since young adolescents' psychosocial development includes the formation of cultural identities, they benefit when educators understand and encourage the development of healthy cultural identities rather than implying that culturally diverse learners should replace cherished cultural beliefs with those of middle class Anglo Americans. In our world where racism, prejudice, and discrimination continue, effective middle level programs must try to instill the value of cultural differences rather than perceiving differences as deficits to be overcome.

Ethnicity

Ethnicity describes groups in which members share a cultural heritage from one generation to another (Pedersen, 1988). Gordon (1964) defines ethnicity as the basis of national origin, religion, and/or race. Ethnicity usually includes such attributes as: a) a group image and sense of identity derived from similar values, behaviors, beliefs, and language; (b) shared political and economic interests; and (c) involuntary membership, although actual identification with that group may be optional (Appleton, 1983; Banks, 1981). Various definitions of ethnicity follow.

- Loyalty to a distinctive cultural pattern related to common ancestry, nation, religion, and/or race (Davis, 1978).

- The sharing of unique and social cultural heritage passed on from generation to generation and based on race, religion, and national identity (Mindel & Habenstein, 1981).

- Identification by distinctive patterns of family life, language, recreation, religion, and other customs that differentiate them from others (Banks, 1991).

Implications of middle level educators understanding ethnicity include: (a) all young adolescents are not alike—individuals' perspectives toward identities, values, and beliefs differ; (b) people from a similar geographical region differ greatly, e.g., people from such countries as Vietnam, Cambodia, Laos, and Thailand differ greatly from the more populous Asian groups, and likewise, differ greatly among themselves (West, 1983); and (c) social class differences, to be addressed later, make considering individual young adolescents' ethnicity even more important since lower, middle, and upper class people of similar ethnicity often differ greatly.

Gender

Gender can be defined as differences in masculinity and femininity—the thoughts, feelings, and behaviors that indicate maleness or femaleness (Gollnick & Chinn, 1990). Societal expectations of acceptable behavior for men and women vary across cultures, but generally speaking, traditional expectations have been for women to be caregivers—gentle, nurturing, and dependent while men are strong and in control of themselves at all times (Davenport & Yurich, 1991).

While efforts during the past decade or so have sought to reduce strict sex role expectations, young adolescents, during these crucial years of developing personal and cultural identities, continue to be faced with sex role expectations. Gender inequities pose other problems:

- educational experiences and school expectations that differ for boys and girls, particularly in science and mathematics;

- textbooks, especially in language arts and social studies that sometimes harbor sex role stereotypes;

- educational practices, e.g., learning and teaching styles, catering to boys; and

- expectations that boys will excel in individual or competitive activities yet expecting girls to excel in nurturing activities (Butler & Sperry, 1991).

While many similarities exist between males and females, gender differences also exist and deserve consideration when planning educational experiences. Research has suggested that there are identifiable differences among young adolescent boys and girls. Some of them are:

1. **Achievement in verbal and mathematics tasks.** At about ten years old, girls excel at verbal tasks; beginning in early adolescence, boys excel at mathematics tasks; between ten and twelve, boys excel on visual/spatial tasks (Gollnick & Chinn, 1990).

2. **Intrapersonal self-esteem.** Boys have higher intrapersonal self-esteem throughout the early adolescence years, i.e., boys feel better about themselves on personal levels while girls feel better in social situations (Madhere, 1991).

3. **Health status and concerns.** Girls associate health status with emotional and social concerns while boys associate physical concerns with health status (Alexander, 1989).

4. **Achievement and self-image.** The relationship between achievement and self-image decreases for girls and increases for boys during the transition to the seventh grade and remains stable as they move into the eighth grade (Roberts, Saragiani, Petersen, & Newman, 1990).

5. **Gender and social networks.** Males and females usually report the same number of best friends; however, attributes considered important in themselves and their same-sex friends differed according to sex, and, last, males have larger social networks than females (Benenson, 1990).

6. **Gender, self-concept and body image.** Generally speaking, boys feel more satisfied with their bodies than females. Changes affecting the female body may have the potential for making a young adolescent female disappointed in her body while the male may be more concerned with task mastery and effectiveness rather than actual physical appearance (Koff, Rierdan, & Stubbs, 1990).

7. **Gender and achievement.** Females when provided curricular choices select fewer mathematics courses than males, probably because counselors and educators rather than females' actual weaknesses or lack of ability steer females away

from mathematics and sciences . When educators reword higher level mathematics to fit female perspectives, females show as much ability as males (Butler & Sperry, 1991).

8. **Gender and sex role attitudes and behaviors.** Findings between sex role attitudes and actual behaviors differed. For example, while both males and females demonstrated highly nontraditional sex role attitudes, females proved significantly more nontraditional in their sex role behaviors. Factors affecting females' sex role attitudes included maternal employment, the level of traditionalism demonstrated by the father, the amount of time the daughter spent with the father, and the father's chronological age (Nelson & Keith, 1990).

Specific suggestions for addressing gender differences and providing gender-appropriate teaching-learning experiences are included in the Challenges section near the end of this chapter.

Social class

Atkinson, Morten, and Sue (1989) maintained that social class differences play significant roles in determining how a person acts, lives, thinks, and relates to others. Differences in values among students and educators basically represent class differences, since many culturally diverse learners come from lower socioeconomic homes and neighborhoods. These social differences and their effects warrant consideration as educators plan educational experiences. Too often, educators use the learners' social class to judge motivation and overall success orientations. Such policies can be a serious mistake, especially when educators assume lower classes lack ambition, experience lower academic achievement, do not want to work, and do not want to improve their educational status. Many Native, African, Asian, and Hispanic Americans (just as many other cultures) want to improve their social status in life but meet with considerable frustration when faced with low education and high unemployment, conditions too often associated with poverty and other lower social class status in U.S. society.

Clear implications surface for middle level educators from these realities. First, using young adolescents' social class level to judge motivation and academic achievement can be a serious error. Just as many middle and upper class young adolescents appear to be unmotivated, many lower class learners appear motivated and determined to succeed. Second, many lower class parents advocate education as a ticket out of poverty. Third, a self-fulfilling prophecy often occurs when educators expect less motivation, limited academic achievement, and less desirable behavior from lower class learners.

Generational

Understanding diversity among young adolescents requires gaining knowledge of generational differences, especially with Asian and Hispanic American learners. Generational differences result in varying beliefs and values, i.e., young adolescents of first generation parents may cling to traditional cultural beliefs. Sons may be valued more than daughters, native languages may be difficult to give up, and teachers may be looked upon with such reverence that parents would never offer suggestions to teachers in parent-teacher conferences. With later generations, some cultural assimilation may have occurred, and young adolescents may have many characteristics similar to the majority culture. Younger generations may be more fluent in English, may be more willing to participate in classroom activities, and may be more willing to consider peers' expectations.

Middle level educators who understand the importance of accepting generation differences recognize the futility in expecting all learners to act alike. Through individualized educational environments, talking one-on-one with individuals, and meeting parents and extended family members, educators recognize the differences among generations and the dangers associated with assuming too much similarity among cultures and learners.

Problems Associated with an Increasingly Culturally Diverse Society

Stereotyping

Stereotyping can be described as the prejudicial attitude of a person or group that superimposes a generalization about behavioral characteristics on a total race, sex, or religion (Lum, 1986). Stereotypes produce an overly general mental picture that usually results in a negative or positive judgmental image of a person or an entire culture. Educators can readily understand the dangers associated with stereotyping, especially when these mental images become the basis for educational decisions and also contribute to people being victims of racism.

One stereotype deserving attention is the negative image of young adolescents themselves. Educators and the general public too often stereotype young adolescents as being difficult to teach and overly preoccupied with the opposite sex when, in actuality, many young adolescents completely defy this stereotype. Other stereotypes include Asian Americans being bright, hard-working, and a model minority or perhaps describing Native Americans as lazy and unmotivated. Stereotyping can be devastating to learners. Educational experiences may reflect erroneous beliefs and thus be too easy or too difficult, may be based upon expectations that certain culturally diverse groups will misbehave, and may predetermine learners' behavior and success in school.

Racism

Signs of racist behavior and racial unrest indicate that "racism is alive and well in the public school" (Stover, 1990, p. 14). Indicators of continuing racism include three students bringing a white doll to school wearing a Ku Klux Klan robe and a black doll with a noose around its neck; racial tensions sparked when several white students displayed Confederate flags during a black history program; and fights erupted between whites and Asian immigrants in a mostly white, affluent neighborhood (Stover, 1990).

Racism can have serious effects on culturally diverse young adolescents. First, culturally diverse learners interpret the actions of others as discriminatory and racist. Second, victims of racism attribute the cause to the person behind the action, to themselves, to social circumstances, or to some combination of the three. Third, they form conclusions about themselves and their self-worth, and make decisions about how they will react to future racist acts. Racism effects learners' academic achievement and self-esteem and fosters apathy and poor perception of future possibilities (Murray & Clark, 1990).

Young adolescents are certainly not immune to racism and may be vulnerable to even more serious consequences. During these transitional years, racism, overt or subtle, can seriously harm self-esteem and cultural identities. At the very time young adolescents are forming identities that may last a lifetime, many of them are aware of racist opinions about their cultural backgrounds.

Institutional racism, another insidious plague, occurs when schools or other organizations serving the public have rules, expectations, and policies that exclude certain populations. One outstanding example, homogeneous ability grouping, all too often results in segregation of learners. Other examples include any organizational arrangement which excludes learners, separates learners by culture or social class, or, as previously mentioned, bases performance expectations on cultural stereotypes.

Prejudice

Allport (1954, 1979) defined prejudice as "feeling, favorable or unfavorable, toward a person or thing which is not based on actual experience." Although prejudice can hold a negative or positive tone, racial and ethnic prejudice in the United States has taken on a primarily negative connotation. Key components of prejudice include being negative in nature and can be individually or group focused; a feeling which can be only an attitude or belief or can be overtly expressed; a belief based on faulty or unsubstantiated data; and an attitude rooted in generalizations. In light of new evidence, the person harboring prejudicial attitudes would be resistant to evidence which would contradict the negative belief (Ponterotto, 1991). As with racism, prejudice can interfere with learner development, school expectations for achievement and behavior, and a host of other negative behaviors. Educators have a responsibility to treat all learners in an objective fashion, to provide equal educational experiences for all learners, and to have objective perceptions and expectations for all learners regardless of cultural, gender, and social class backgrounds.

Students at Foss High School in Tacoma, Washington began a "Breakfast Club" to foster better understanding among students of different cultural backgrounds. Club members spend four to six hours a month being trained in prejudice reduction and conflict resolution. Recently, the club organized a multicultural conference that included sessions on sexual harassment, African American storytelling, Pacific Island dances, the Holocaust, and what it means to be Asian ("Breakfast club creates understanding...," 1994).

Crimes of hate

Hate crimes increasingly place young adolescents in precarious situations. Hate crimes can include obscene messages against ethnic, racial, and religious groups; verbal abuse and threats; and words and deeds motivated by negative feelings and opinions about a victim's race, ethnicity, and/or religion. Hate crimes are currently soaring at record-breaking rates throughout the nation. Hate crimes may seem different from other assaults only in terms of their motivation; however, some characteristics of hate crimes are relatively rare in other crimes of violence. Characteristics of hate crimes include:

- perpetrators of hate crimes and the victim may be total strangers;

- perpetrators often assault a single victim;

- perpetrators often attack younger or weaker victims and often arm themselves to attack unarmed victims;

- perpetrators usually engage in extremely violent crimes and inflict serious injuries;

- perpetrators often destroy or damage property rather than take something of value;

- perpetrators usually fail to gain anything of material value from the assault; and

- perpetrators frequently engage in hate crimes at churches, synagogues, mosques, cemeteries, monuments, schools, camps, and in or around the victim's home (Bodinger-deUriarte, 1991).

Hate crimes are caused by bigotry; the unbearable sense of personal failure that leads people to avoid self-blame by scapegoating others; the feeling of power gained by subjugating others; the feeling of superiority gained by by dehumanizing others; and other causes resulting from social unease, economic unease, and political unease (Bodinger-deUriarte, 1991).

Middle level schools undoubtedly need to be safe places. *Turning Points* (Carnegie Council of Adolescent Development, 1989) takes a strong stand on providing safe schools:

> Above all, schools must be safe places. The changes in middle grades schools suggested in this report, by creating an ethos of mutual support and responsibility, should greatly reduce the conflicts and tensions among youth that lead to violence (p. 66).

Educators can work toward safe and orderly environments by having strong leadership at the building and district levels, modeling respect for all people, having clear and enforceable rules, and implementing programs designed to involve parents and extended family members.

Historical and institutional barriers

Historical barriers include the dual school system which segregated learners by race, the Jim Crow laws once prevalent in the South, and an educational system which often had (and in some cases, continues to have) lower expectations for culturally diverse learners. Institutional barriers include ability grouping, educational practices leading to exclusivity and lack of equal access, and the belief that only certain students should play leading or significant roles in schools. While the latter barriers may be unintentional, the result remains the same—individuals are prohibited from participating and experiencing success in all school activities.

Educators can work to reduce barriers by countering the belief that African Americans should play particular sports and Asian Americans should comprise the majority of the computer club membership. Other barriers include limiting cheerleading teams to ten or eleven students when a thousand or more might attend the school; requiring students to choose elective areas when students demonstrate talents in several areas; and placing students in low ability groups which often use the least effective instructional methods.

All young adolescents need opportunities to be involved and participate in activities and programs that are open to other students. Schools allowing exclusivity practices which "weed-out" students fail in their educational effort, often citing excuses or refusing to accept blame for barriers to participation. Efforts involving all young adolescents in academic programs and extracurricular activities reflect the concept of equal access.

Challenges for Middle Level Schools in a Multicultural Society

Middle level educators working to improve the lives of young adolescents in the years ahead will face at least five challenges, each of which will be addressed on the following pages.

Addressing the problems affecting urban learners

While one must carefully avoid overgeneralizing about urban learners and avoid blaming victims for their plight, several studies (Grant, 1989; Maeroff, 1988; "Urban eighth graders," 1993) suggest many urban students do not receive appropriate educational experiences while other students do. Also, for various reasons, many urban students do not take advantage of educational opportunities which do exist, and subsequently, fail to meet academic achievement routinely expected in both rural and suburban schools.

One report revealed learners lacked a sense of belonging to the school and did not perceive a connection between school work and the world outside the school; lacked motivation and perceived little reason for attending school; demonstrated atrocious attendance habits; engaged in low-level schoolwork with the teachers demonstrating low expectations for learner achievement; and failed to understand their lack of academic progress in schoolwork (Maeroff, 1988).

Culturally diverse learners are usually the hardest hit among urban learners. While our nation ranks consistently below other developed nations in international comparisons of educational performance, our bottom half is far worse. For the most part, the bottom half consists of poor and culturally diverse learners, and many, particularly those trapped in the inner cities of the largest urban areas, are increasingly locked into an underclass from which escape seems hopeless (Miller, 1992). One study revealed a widening gap in eighth graders students' performance in reading achievement between high and low poverty schools. Specifically, urban disadvantaged eighth graders averaged only 3% correct answers on questions requiring extended answers, compared to 85% for all eighth graders ("Urban eighth graders," 1993).

Grant (1989) suggests that the economic and social plight of urban culturally diverse students has grown more acute because of high joblessness rates, mother-only households, welfare dependency, out-of-wedlock births, and crime. Unlike students from advantaged schools who are able to see the benefits of delayed gratification, urban learners often have difficulty waiting for rewards (Maeroff, 1988).

Miller (1992) describes the realities of urban schools: run-down buildings, poor attendance, illiteracy, high dropout rates, vandalism and violence, low expectations, despair, and hopelessness. Urban schools are often large, impersonal places where students lack a sense of belonging and do not see a connection between classroom activities and their lives. Demands and expectations for attendance and academic achievement placed upon urban students fail to achieve desired educational efforts (Maeroff, 1988).

Students in large cities, who suffer the worst educationally, also experience both problem-laden schools and the ills peculiar to urban life. An array of problems surround many urban schools: support services unable to address urban learners' needs, the cycle of life on welfare being insufficient to meet family needs or promote self-sufficiency, job training programs unable to reduce unemployment, and poor housing situations (Maeroff, 1988).

The gloomy picture painted of urban learners and schools also holds true for some urban teachers. While undoubtedly many excellent teachers teach in urban schools, some urban teachers lack knowledge of pedagogical methods necessary to address the needs of urban learners; fail to understand the problems and challenges faced by urban learners; present unchallenging and sometimes boring curricular experiences; and set low expectations for learner achievement (Grant, 1989).

Also, some teachers, perhaps born after the Civil Rights movement, have only a textbook understanding of equality and justice (Grant, 1989). Teachers lacking this understanding or perceiving differences as threatening will be unlikely candidates for providing effective educational and social experiences for urban learners (Haberman, 1991).

The urban schools research suggests several directions for improving innercity middle schools:

1. Urban learners can achieve both academically and behaviorally when teachers consider children capable of learning, provide challenging curricula and instruction, and demonstrate appropriate teaching strategies (Oakes, 1987). Specific conditions that contribute to the effective learning of urban students include being helped to understand major concepts, ideas, and general principles rather than studying only isolated facts; being involved in planning learning activities; being actively involved in real-life experiences; being involved with the technology of information access; and working in heterogeneous groups (Haberman, 1991).

2. Urban teachers demonstrate positive attitudes and enthusiasm with urban students when professional preparation programs provide a thorough knowledge of student characteristics, learning theory, teaching strategies, curricular materials, and a strong commitment to creating democratic learning environments (Stewart, 1991).

3. Urban students need instruction in higher order, problem-solving and critical thinking skills in addition to basic skills instruction. Providing urban learners with thinking opportunities requires that educators move beyond the all-too-common practice of worksheets and practice drills focusing on isolated skill deficiencies (Larkin, 1993). Other opportunities include debates, panel discussions, and role-playing that allow learners to analyze, interpret and apply information, define

issues and problems, prioritize, anticipate possible outcomes, choose options, make decisions, and replan, if necessary (Stewart, 1991).

4. Urban learners benefit when paired with exemplary adults in a mentoring process. While the roles a mentor adopts depends upon the student and the individual situation, a mentor in an urban school can be a person of greater expertise who teaches, counsels, and helps a student. The mentoring function can include providing the student with information, assistance, counseling, protection, and challenges. Successes can be emphasized and friendships and trust can be developed (Fehr, 1993). Students most likely to benefit from mentoring programs include learners passing only half their classes, whose behavior problems tend to result in detentions rather than suspension or expulsion from school, and who receive little support at home. Students falling below these guidelines rarely can have their greater needs met by mentoring programs. They need both professional counseling and more in-depth remediation (Fehr, 1993).

5. Urban students should be expected to maintain high expectations for both achievement and behavior. Several studies (Grant, 1989; Haberman, 1991; Maeroff, 1988) suggest urban schools have low expectations for learner achievement and behavior. Even some urban students complain that their curriculum fails to provide challenges and express the need for more rigorous courses (Grant, 1989). Teachers often face a dilemma because students' lack of success in previous grades continues to contribute to their academic demise. A teacher with high expectations for academic achievement might be setting up students for frustration and failure. A teacher with too low expectations implies that urban students are incapable of performing academic work and dooms them to additional failure (Maeroff, 1988).

Utilizing teaching behaviors appropriate for multicultural settings

For many years, educators planned curricular and instructional experiences primarily for mainstream learners. Little thought was given to culturally diverse learners' learning styles, perceptions of success and motivation, or need for friendship and social interaction. Increasingly, educators are realizing the need for teaching-learning experiences that reflect an understanding of the way culturally diverse learners perceive, think, learn, and socialize. Essentially, both curricular content and teaching behaviors should involve students applying ideals such as fairness, equity, realization of human differences, and justice to their everyday lives (Haberman, 1991). The following inset depicts a number of teaching behaviors that have proven to be effective with multiculturally diverse learners.

Selected Teacher Behaviors
Effective in Multicultural Classrooms

1. Providing learning experiences which reflect how learners' culture influences perceptions of competition, group welfare, sharing, motivation and success. For example, some Native American learners may favor sharing and helping peers over competitive learning activities (Sanders, 1987) and Puerto Ricans may not wish to excel or be set apart from the group as being different (Christensen, 1989).

2. Providing learning experiences which reflect gender differences. Two examples are confronting gender bias in curricular materials and encouraging gender integration through peer tutoring and other small learning groups (Sadker, Sadker & Long, 1993) and encouraging open dialogue and collaboration (Butler & Sperry, 1991).

3. Providing learning experiences which reflect culturally diverse learners' learning styles. For instance, some African Americans prefer to respond to things in terms of the whole picture rather than its parts and also tend to approximate space, numbers, and time rather than striving for accuracy (Hale-Benson, 1986).

4. Encouraging and supporting the development of bilingual programs (Crawford, 1993).

5. Immersing students in print and varied oral language activities that are meaningful, relevant, and functional in a pluralistic society (Crawford, 1993).

6. Treating all students with fairness—the ability to establish a democratic classroom wherein all students are treated equitably (Sadker & Sadker, 1982).

7. Expecting all students to succeed academically rather than automatically expecting minority students to perform less well academically (Garcia, 1984).

8. Using heterogeneous grouping whenever possible to enhance self-esteem and promote inter-ethnic interaction (Gollnick & Chinn, 1990).

9. Demonstrating the necessity of democratic values and attitudes, a multicultural education philosophy, and an ability to view events and situations from diverse ethnic perspectives and points of view (Banks, 1981).

10. Recognizing the belief that culturally diverse parents and families do not care about their children's education is a myth with serious consequences (Chavkin, 1989).

11. Encouraging cross-cultural friendships and social interaction, cooperation, and socialization among boys and girls of all cultures at school, on the playground, and in the community.

12. Addressing the special problems which culturally diverse parents and families may face such as language difficulties and misunderstanding the U.S. school system and its expectations.

13. Having factual knowledge about learner differences such as culture, race, ethnicity, social class, and gender and the professional commitment to have educational experiences reflect these differences.

14. Encouraging and arranging classrooms that reflect cultural diversity via bulletin boards, walls, artwork, artifacts.

15. Encouraging students to work in cooperative groups and other cross-cultural arrangements to allow social interaction, conversation, and meaningful dialogue.

Recognize the effects of cultural differences on academic achievement and socialization

Middle level educators will be challenged to recognize cultural and often related gender differences and to provide multicultural education programs and educational experiences that reflect these differences. Four considerations related to cultural differences follow.

1. Forming personal and ethnic identities is a central task during early adolescence. For example, African American eighth graders think about and discuss their ethnic group membership and generally focus on their own ethnic group (Phinney & Tarver, 1988).

2. Young adolescents experience a changing self-concept which is affected by one's cultural and racial perceptions as well as their perceptions of how others feel about them. Asian and Pacific Islander children's physical and racial self-concepts appear to be more negative than their Anglo American counterparts. Japanese Americans score slightly lower than Anglo American children on all self-concept scores (Pang et al., 1985).

3. Many Native Americans demonstrate strengths in visual/spatial/perceptual information; use imagery to remember concepts and words (mental associations assist in remembering); demonstrate tendencies toward being reflective rather than impulsive, or watch-then-do rather than trial and error; and exhibit tendencies toward participating in global processing on both verbal and nonverbal tasks (More, 1987).

4. African Americans perceive their environment in its entirety rather than in isolated parts; prefer intuitive rather than deductive or inductive reasoning; approximate concepts of space, number and time rather than aim at exactness or accuracy (Shade, 1982).

In order to ensure educational experiences which are culturally appropriate teachers should provide:

- cooperative learning, multicultural education, and positive classroom management practices (Deegan, 1992);

- teaching strategies which foster student thought, encourage risk-taking, focus on student knowledge, and encourage open dialogue, collaboration, and involvement (Butler & Sperry, 1991);

- educational experiences which reflect females' developmental differences;

- recognition that learners of a particular culture may react differently to a given situation due to acculturation, social class, generational, and developmental differences;

- activities which contribute to the development of positive cultural, masculine, and feminine identities;

- providing teaching-learning experiences which recognize the relationship between gender, self-concept, and body image; and

- providing both boys and girls with instruction designed to teach them about their developing bodies (Manning, 1993b).

Providing gender-appropriate educational experiences

Why is addressing young adolescents' gender differences important? During early adolescence boys and girls form overall gender identities and specific role behaviors which may determine attitudes and behaviors for a lifetime. General approaches for ensuring gender-appropriate teaching-learning experiences include emphasizing females' accomplishments in addition to those of males, directing questions to girls as well as boys, selecting curricular materials which avoid sexist connotations, recognizing developmental differences between boys and girls, and planning gender-appropriate instructional experiences. More specific suggestions for providing gender equitable educational experiences include:

1. A social studies lesson can address the important roles women of all cultural backgrounds played in the Western movement; describe reasons for Anglo women and African American women wanting to move west and the reasons for Native American and Mexican women resisting the Western movement; identify evidence of sexism during the movement and compare with the sexism today; and identify and discuss differences in the culture and roles of pioneer women and Native American women.

2. A language arts and social studies lesson (grades 5-8) can focus on "Resisting and Surviving Slavery" by describing the lives of females slaves, how they resisted slavery, and how women other than slaves fought the practice of slavery.

3. A vocal music lesson can identify genres of contemporary music and then focus specifically on portrayal of sex roles and gender relationships; analyze peer-group norms for sex roles and gender relationships; and write or listen to contemporary nonsexist music selections (Grant & Sleeter, 1989).

4. An integrated curricular approach can be used to study women who have contributed to U.S. history: Queen Liluokalani—Hawaii's first reigning queen and nationalist; Molly Pitcher's and Deborah Sampson's contributions during the Revolutionary War; Clara Barton of the Civil War, and other notable women such as Dorothea Dix, Jane Addams, Eleanor Roosevelt, and Mary McLeod Bethune (Tetreault, 1993).

5. Strategies to avoid males dominating classroom discussions can be used. For instance, teachers can become more aware of the degree and type of attention they give members of each sex in the classroom and, then, make the necessary adjustments; they can make adjustments to treat the sexes equally in the number of comments when offering acceptance, praise, remediation or criticism; they should avoid letting class "stars" dominate learner-teacher interactions; they can call upon students in an equitable manner by ignoring boys speaking out of turn and calling upon students in a systematic manner (e.g. calling upon students alphabetically, skipping every second or third name, and following learners' birthdays chronologically, Stanford, 1992).

6. Strategies employed in classrooms where gender differences were not evident in girls' and boys' scores may include: (1) teachers expected boys and girls to be orderly and businesslike; (2) teachers offered less praise and criticism to both girls and boys; (3) teachers ensured equal student participation; (4) teachers interacted with students more individually; and (5) teachers conducted fewer whole class drills (Stanford, 1992).

7. Strategies strengthening girls' entry into early adolescence may include teachers realizing their unique opportunities to assist young adolescent girls; teachers examining models of adult women worthy of portrayal and becoming models for young adolescent girls to emulate; teachers encouraging and openly valuing young adolescent girls' thinking; and teachers encouraging girls to express their ideas and to risk disagreeing with others (Stanford, 1992).

8. Health and physical education strategies may include addressing girls' concerns about their health status as well as their emotional and social concerns. Their concerns should be considered equally important to boys' concerns and should be addressed by a person qualified in both young adolescent development and competent to understand females' concerns and perspectives.

9. In cooperative learning groups, emphasis on equal social interaction and participation as well as an atmosphere of cooperation rather than competition should be encouraged.

10. Girls can be provided opportunities to work with the friends they select. These opportunities can include making key decisions, working cooperatively to-

ward agreed-upon goals, assigning roles for each participant, and selecting topics which have particular relevance to young women.

Recognizing and addressing language diversity

Language diversity has in some aspects divided the nation and has contributed to the failure of schools to provide an adequate education for culturally diverse learners. In many schools, learners and their families speak a staggering number of languages, as the languages of Central and South America, Africa, and Asia combine with the various American dialects. Language-minority learners often fail to learn the essential lessons of school, and do not fully participate in the economic, social, and political life of the United States. The problem for language-minority learners and their educators will grow even more serious over the next decade or two as language-minority children and adolescents become the majority in public schools (Bowman, 1989).

While some progress has been made toward appreciating language diversity, even today some educators punish learners for speaking their native languages or send notes to parents who can barely speak English, asking them not to speak their native language with their children. Such practices demonstrate the magnitude of the language problem (Nieto, 1992).

Dialect, and the issue of whether to require standard English in schools, is both a very sensitive and controversial issue. Since dialects are often considered nonstandard, this issue has civil rights implications. Requiring students to speak standard English in schools may be considered discriminatory by some, who believe such a requirement places additional educational burdens on non-standard English speaking students. Also, the insistence on standard English may hinder the acquisition of other educational skills, making it difficult for these students to succeed. One can reasonably argue that such a practice denies limited-English-speaking students the same educational opportunities as others, and thus morally, if not legally, denies them their civil rights (Gollnick & Chinn, 1990).

Learners speaking English as a second language also challenge educators. The language diversity that exists in the United States extends itself into the schools, and in large urban and metropolitan school districts there may be nearly a hundred different languages spoken. While some students are bilingual in English and their native language, others either do not speak English, or have limited English speaking skills. Furthermore, indications suggest the number of students with limited English speaking skills will increase (Gollnick & Chinn, 1990). Some culturally diverse learners are quite competent in English; however, others may speak only Spanish, the second most common language in the U.S.; one of the many Asian languages; or a less common language such as Arabic or Tongian (Haring, 1990).

In light of this reality, it is important that teachers hold appropriate perceptions of language diversity such as seeing language diversity as positive rather than negative, recognizing that language discrimination has played a key role in our history, and not viewing negatively programs for linguistically diverse students (Nieto, 1992).

Strategies conveying the importance of language include:

- encouraging students to use their native languages with language peers, both in academic and social situations;

- pairing students with a friend more fluent in English and encouraging each to teach the other;

- motivating students to teach peers about their language and culture; and

- inviting guests who speak a variety of languages to the classroom (Nieto, 1992).

A more extensive section on how language diversity is a multicultural issue and effective strategies for teaching linguistically different learners can be found in Chapter 4.

Summary

Our increasingly multicultural society provides additional challenges for educators, especially middle level educators who teach young adolescents during the crucial developmental years when psychosocial and intellectual development allows perspectives toward others to be formed. Accepting the demographics of a changing population, understanding the many forms of diversity, recognizing and being willing to address the problems plaguing our culturally diverse society loom as prerequisites to providing effective multicultural education programs. Middle level educators who meet the challenges of teaching in increasingly culturally diverse classrooms will make middle level schools more democratic and may even make a contribution toward ultimately improving the world. ◆

2

Multicultural Education

Children of all nations are alike, until adults teach them.

CHAPTER OUTLINE

Multicultural Education   **2**

S everal factors suggest the need for middle level schools to make an affirmative response to help culturally diverse learners succeed in school and to help majority-culture learners recognize and appreciate differences among people. First, as Chapter 1 detailed, our nation continues to become more culturally diverse. Second, young adolescents' psychosocial and cognitive development allows learners to understand diversity among people and to form long-standing attitudes about others. Third, educators increasingly understand the effects of culture on self-esteem, academic achievement, and overall development. Fourth, the multicultural education movement and the middle school movement share similarities—both focus on the overall welfare of learners. While several textbooks (Banks, 1992; Baruth & Manning, 1992; Gollnick & Chinn, 1990; Hernandez, 1989) examine the concept and process of multicultural education, this chapter examines multicultural education specifically from a middle school perspective.

Multicultural Education in Culturally Pluralistic Schools

Multicultural education, a relatively new concept, was not listed as an identifying term in the *Education Index* until 1978. The last decade, however, has seen considerable emphasis, both in the literature and in practical application, on providing multicultural education programs in schools (Tiedt & Tiedt, 1990). Three forces contributed to the emergence of the multicultural education program: the Civil Rights movement brought awareness of cultural differences and the need for social change; critics scrutinized school textbooks for stereotypical images, misrepresentations, and outright omissions; and cultural differences began to be considered as enriching rather than as deficits to be eliminated (Gay, 1983).

By the late 1960s, the movement had matured into an energetic coalition joining many culturally diverse groups who directed attention toward determination and power. Likewise, leaders sought changes in school system, i.e., segregation in some geographical areas and a curricula which focused primarily on Anglo perspectives. And educators began to recognize the need to address culturally diverse learners' strengths, weaknesses, and learning styles and to teach respect and acceptance for all learners (Sleeter & Grant, 1988).

During the 1970s, multicultural educators adopted a more comprehensive approach and examined diversity of all kinds: culture, ethnicity, language, gender, handicaps, and social class (Hernandez, 1989). Emphasis since the 1970s has focused on changing educational institutions and the overall society from singular-minded Anglo perspectives to a more egalitarian mindset recognizing diversity as enriching and cultural differences as strengths on which to build.

During the 1980s, a powerful interest emerged in multicultural education and has continued to the present. Educators began to realize that, while the major Civil Rights movement of the 1960s contributed to much-needed social improvements, considerable changes continued to be needed as new racial incidents resurfaced (if incidents ever stopped), and, generally speaking, culturally diverse people had not made the social progress many expected. Affirmative action programs had contributed to increased job opportunities, and efforts to integrate previously segregated housing areas succeeded to some extent. While notable progress has been made, however, much remains to be done.

Considerable evidence suggests the late 1980s and early 1990s were significant times for multicultural education: books began to clarify the concept and to offer suggestions; a flurry of journal articles appeared; schools began deliberate efforts to change philosophy and practice to reflect diversity; and educators began to recognize the effect of diversity on self-esteem, academic achievement, and overall development.

Definitions

The term, "multicultural education," has different meanings for different people. Admittedly, such differences often contribute to confusion when planning and implementing programs. The approach educators take probably reflects their definition and their respective school situation rather than disagreements concerning the actual need for multicultural education. Sufficient similarities do exist, however, for educators to implement curricular, instructional, and environmental practices that recognize and respect cultural diversity. Two definitions that illustrate the commitment to the education and overall welfare of all people follow:

> Multicultural education is a reform movement that is trying to change the schools and other educational institutions so that students from all social class, gender, racial and cultural groups will have an equal opportunity to learn (Banks & Banks, 1993, p. 4).

> A multicultural perspective is a recognition of (1) the so-
> cial, political, and economic realities that individuals experi-
> ence in culturally diverse and complex human encounters, and
> (2) the importance of culture, race, sex, and gender, ethnicity,
> socio-economic status, and exceptionalities in the education
> process (NCATE, 1986, p. 47).

An adequate definition of multicultural education in middle level schools, both
as a concept and a process, needs to reflect the basic philosophy of middle level
education and the unique developmental needs of young adolescents.

**Multicultural education in middle level education is both a concept and a
deliberate process designed to:**

- **teach young adolescents to recognize, accept, and appreciate cultural,
  ethnic, social class, religious, and gender differences among people; and**

- **instill in young adolescents during their crucial psychosocial and cognitive developmental period a sense of responsibility and a commitment to
  work toward the democratic ideals of justice, equality, and democracy.**

Program goals

Banks (1992) advanced the position that is an emerging consensus on a common goal of multicultural education. Banks proposed, "the consensus centers around
a primary goal for multicultural education, which is to increase educational equality for both gender groups, for students from diverse ethnic and cultural groups,
and for exceptional students" (p. 24).

The basic premise of this monograph could be stated in the following sentence:

**Simply providing educational equity will not suffice—responsive
multicultural education programs must also encourage all young adolescents
to work toward democratic values, justice, equality, and democracy for all
people as well as take responsible action to reduce the harmful effects of racism, prejudice, and discrimination.**

Thinking only of young adolescents and middle level education, what goals
might educators specifically adopt in developing multicultural education programs?

1. Adopt a perspective of multicultural education reflecting the essentials of
effective middle level education and also reflecting the belief that early adolescence is a crucial time to teach about differences among people.

2. Provide multicultural educational experiences which address 10-14 year olds' psychosocial and cognitive development characteristics such as their cultural identities and changing self-esteems.

3. Incorporate multiculturalism in all middle school programs such as exploratory courses, teacher advisory groups, and integrated curricular units.

4. Empower young adolescents and their educators to understand and respect their own and others' cultural backgrounds.

5. Select organization patterns (i.e., learning teams, school-within-a-school, and cooperative learning groups) that reflect cultural, gender, and social class differences.

6. Organize community service projects that provide significant service opportunities and show young adolescents the satisfaction and benefits derived from rendering service.

7. Ensure that special support professionals such as speech therapists and counselors understand the problems culturally diverse young adolescents are likely to face.

8. Ensure the understanding that culturally diverse learners' cultural perceptions of motivation may differ as may the importance they place on time.

Multicultural education programs will be more effective when educators consider these goals. Other considerations affecting program responsiveness include degree of diversity, racial unrest in the school and community, and the school's overall commitment.

Fundamental principles

Providing appropriate multicultural education requires more than simply teaching cultural facts about groups of people and their contributions to society. Several fundamental principles make multicultural education programs more effective.

First, multicultural education programs and the middle school program complement each other. Therefore, rather than considering them as two distinct programs, efforts should be focused toward building the two together in such a way that the strengths of one complement the other.

Second, curricular materials complement learners' cultural diversity as well as their developmental levels. For example, carefully-selected tradebooks for libraries and reading tables would have reading and interest levels appropriate for learners' cognitive and academic achievement levels and portray culturally diverse youngsters in roles other than stereotypical images.

Third, multicultural efforts in middle schools make it evident that multiculturalism is not just rhetoric but reality. Questions such as the following need to be addressed in following this principle. How many culturally diverse faculty members, administrators, and support service personnel work at the school?

What are the attitudes and perceptions of culturally diverse learners? Are extracurricular activities segregated or nearly segregated by race? What type music is played at parties and sock hops? Is art created by artists from various cultures valued and received enthusiastically by educators?

Fourth, culture influences the way students cognitively process information (Cordova and Love (1987). Cultural and gender differences influence learning styles, motivation, socialization, and other factors affecting school achievement.

Knowledge, attitudes, and skills

The success of multicultural education programs, regardless of their lofty and ambitious goals, will depend upon the knowledge, attitudes, and skills educators bring to daily educational situations and social interactions. Knowledge of cultures, attitudes toward diversity, and the skills to work with culturally diverse learners will determine a program's effectiveness in promoting harmony.

Knowledge. During the past several decades, the professional literature on multicultural education has increased dramatically and enhanced educators' knowledge of cultural diversity. Educators now have access to valuable objective information describing various culturally diverse groups. No longer need decisions concerning learners' education be based on inaccurate and stereotypical generalizations. For example, knowledgeable educators understand Native Americans' concept of sharing, African Americans' unique language, Asian Americans' concept of generational and family relationships, and Hispanic Americans' belief in machismo and commitment to the Spanish language. Equally important is the understanding that these characteristics may or may not hold true with each culturally diverse learner and may vary with generation, socioeconomic status, and geographical location (Baruth & Manning, 1992).

Attitudes. Knowledge of how cultural diversity enriches our society is a prerequisite to the development of effective multicultural education programs. However, the attitudes of educators toward accepting others and their differences is without doubt a second prerequisite. Knowledge does not necessarily imply acceptance or a positive attitude toward others. Multicultural education programs that make a difference in young adolescents' lives are operated by faculty that do recognize diversities as strengths on which to build curricular decisions, instructional methods, and classroom environments.

Other attitudinal aspects include accepting unique cognitive, psychosocial, linguistic, and sociocultural capabilities young adolescents bring to learning situations; believing that all learners deserve, ethically and legally, equal access to all learning opportunities; and viewing racism, prejudice, and discrimination as evils to be addressed.

Attitudes also include people progressing from ethnocentrism (the belief in the superiority of one's culture) to valuing differences, having an understanding of how their cultural attitudes affect the learning process, and having accepted the differences between learners and themselves. Not easily hoodwinked, young adolescents are a perceptive group and can detect when educators teach acceptance and positive attitudes yet continue to harbor negative feelings and to perpetuate practices that often segregate learners.

Skills. Although having both knowledge and appropriate attitudes is of paramount importance, possessing the skills needed to teach and relate to culturally diverse learners is also crucial. Skills include responding appropriately to learners' strengths and weaknesses; addressing areas needing remediation; responding to the relationship between learners' orientations toward school and academic success; selecting standardized tests and evaluation instruments with the least cultural bias; and utilizing teaching methods that have proven especially appropriate for culturally diverse young adolescents. Also needed is the ability to understand and respond appropriately to the concerns of culturally diverse learners and to arrange for appropriate school and community resources for learners needing specialized assistance.

A comprehensive approach: curriculum, instruction, and environment

Middle level educators have long recognized that tinkering with curricular, instructional, and environmental practices often results in few genuine improvements. The comprehensive reform movement currently underway bids to affect nearly every aspect of middle level education. Just as improving middle level schools requires considerable effort, so the planning and implementing of effective multicultural education programs require more than cosmetic or superficial changes.

A major premise of this monograph holds that genuine multiculturalism efforts must permeate all facets of middle schoolers' day. Teachers planning an occasional multicultural education activity or unit probably have honorable intentions. However, providing comprehensive curricular experiences, instructional practices, and overall environments that reflect multiculturalism reaps greater benefits. Such an effort makes multiculturalism an integral aspect of the school, a natural and accepted element in the daily routine.

A true multicultural curriculum integrates cultural content throughout subjects and grade levels, placing new content in pedagogically—and contextually—appropriate locations. Such infusion calls for a review of the entire curriculum and will affect all faculty. Restructuring the curriculum to reflect multicultural perspectives requires reconceptualizing our base of knowledge rather than superficially interspersing selected culturally diverse heroes or events into an otherwise unreconstructed curriculum (Diaz, 1992). A one-shot multicultural unit designed to coincide with Black History Week fails to show the importance of diversity. Looking at African Americans only from slavery perspectives and examining slavery only from the plantation owner's perspective shows learners that the school's focus and environment continue to emphasize single-minded perspectives.

Effective instructional approaches reflect culturally diverse learners' learning styles, tendencies toward sharing, motivation, harmony, and cooperation rather than competition. Equally important, grouping students heterogeneously leads to an integration of cultures and increased interethnic social interactions. However, teachers and administrators may not always have absolute control of grouping situations. Realistically speaking, some geographical areas are not populated with representatives of diverse cultural groups. In these areas, whether the school population is primarily culturally diverse or Anglo, educators have few grouping options. However, the need to deal positively with multicultural education exists and must be met.

The degree to which the total classroom environment reflects multiculturalism will determine the success of multicultural education efforts. All courses and programs, all efforts to improve cultural identities and self-concepts, convey respect and acceptance of cultural diversity.

Making multiculturalism a national issue—the Canadian experience

Advocates of multicultural education can look toward Canada where multiculturalism has been a major effort and the interests and needs of pluralistic advocacy groups have been addressed. Canada's provincial school system results in ten slightly different school systems; however, all systems are required to have policies and practice promoting multiculturalism. Federal and provincial offices work to assure that all learners have rights to biculturalism and bilingualism. Designated offices responsible for promoting multicultural education, sometimes referred to as anti-racism education, provide financial resources for cultural and educational activities. Legal mandates require all schools to have a policy promoting multiculturalism. Consultants assist with the implementation of programs by securing materials, hiring minority personnel, and arranging for inservice opportunities (R. Cuthbertson, personal communication, March 22, 1993).

The introduction of Canada's official policy on multiculturalism in 1971 and the Charter of Rights and Freedoms in 1982, which guarantees equality of rights, encouraged such diverse groups as women, the handicapped, and various ethnic groups to demand that schools consider their special needs and aspirations (VanBalkom, 1991). Canada's Federal Commission on Bilingualism and Biculturalism confronted Canada's true nature, i.e., its mosaic of many cultures and ethnic groups. As a result, an official federal policy on multiculturalism was formulated which greatly influenced the institutions and lives of Canadians. The policy stated that Canada would support all its cultures and seek to assist the development of cultural groups that demonstrated a desire and effort to contribute to Canada. The policy also included removal of discriminatory barriers erected against members of culturally diverse groups, promoted creative encounters between ethnic communities, and sought to alleviate prejudice on the basis of race, creed, culture, or belief (Friesen & Wieler, 1988).

The goals of Canada's multiculturalism efforts included reinforcing positive attitudes among people already holding such attitudes, promoting positive attitudes among people not respecting diversity, and creating a social climate that changes negative attitudes. Such actions included sensitizing the general public to the needs of culturally diverse groups and beginning positive action toward respect and appreciation of differences. Likewise, the policy included helping ethnocultural groups to feel that their heritages are valued by the Canadian people and government. The rationale for such action included strong evidence suggesting a need for public education on multiculturalism: Canada's good will toward multiculturalism did not always translate from principle to actual program support; and many Canadians confused multiculturalism with immigration and refugee issues and did not understand how multiculturalism might affect Canada economically, socially, politically, and culturally; and the seriousness of intergroup conflict suggested Canada needed to educate the public as an investment in long-term harmony (Rothman, et al., 1988).

The principles underlying Canada's multicultural program include:

- adopting a multi-faceted approach designed to convey consistent fundamental themes;

- raising public awareness, informing people about the content of the multicultural effort, and bringing people of various ethnocultural backgrounds closer together;

- identifying target groups (and their group interests) within the larger society and stressing the benefits of cultural pluralism;

- considering the differences in the ways multicultural issues are perceived in Quebec and the other parts of Canada; and

- providing an intensive, sustained, and well-coordinated program (Rothman, et al., 1988).

Canada's overall objective and commitment included developing "new policy based on the realities of today and the expectations of tomorrow" (Department of the Secretary of State, 1987, p. 23). The seriousness of Canada's commitment to multiculturalism can be seen in its proposing the establishment of the House Standing Committee on Multiculturalism; convening the first national conference on urban multicultural societies; holding the first federal-provincial-territorial conference of ministers responsible for multiculturalism; and including the Employment Equity Act of 1986, which required federally regulated employers to provide improved access to employment opportunities for women, the disabled, and minority groups (Department of The Secretary of State, 1987)

Promoting bilingualism—the Canadian experience

Unlike the U.S. with only one semi-official language, Canada has two national languages, English and French. Because multiculturalism receives such a high priority in addition to French and English, many school boards offer language classes during the afternoons in learners' native languages, i.e., Korean or Vietnamese (Ralph Cuthbertson, personal communication, March 22, 1993).

Duquette (1987) explained the existing language situation of French Canadians in Manitoba, Ontario, Quebec, and the Maritime provinces by highlighting historical, political, socioeconomic, and education aspects of bilingualism in Canada.

Historically, the first half of Canada's European-based history was under French rule. Today, two influences provide promise for further developing the bilingual character of Canada: the deep French historical roots and the open and favorable climate toward enriching bilingualism. While these two influences will have an effect, three other possibilities downplay the possibility of an enriched bilingual character for Canada. First, Canada borders on the U.S., whose culture and English language dominate business, the media, and most areas of publication and entertainment. Second, the immigration rate into Canada adds to the possibility that Canada will become multilingual and multicultural before it becomes fully bilingual and bicultural. Third, the French Canadians are decreasing in number in proportion to the increasing growth of Canada.

Politically, there has been an increase in political will and determination in implementing bilingual programs designed to serve French Canadians in their own language. Politicians have become increasingly conscious of the importance given to winning politically in Quebec in order to gain a greater majority and also to be more truly representative nationally. As a result of these bilingual programs, Canadians have become more conscious of the realities of Canada and of their distinctiveness as Canadians. These effects have been particularly felt in provinces such as Ontario and New Brunswick that have large populations of French Canadians and border on Quebec.

Socioeconomically, bilingualism is considered an asset in Canada; however, the extent of the positive feelings depends on the province. Because of an economic rivalry between Western Canada and Ontario, Western Canada has never really accepted bilingualism due to the political advantages apparent in Quebec. The Eastern provinces have appeared more tolerant in their attitudes, probably because New Province, a bilingual province, exists in their midst. In Ontario, with the advent of the new liberal government, French language services continue to be extended. Overall, while some people continue to be concerned with protecting the French language, the general population now appears eager to learn English.

Educationally, the demand for French (primarily French language schools and immersion programs) continues to be a high priority among Canadians. In Ontario and other parts of Canada where numbers warrant, the pressure for French immersion by English speaking parents continues to be very strong. Also, efforts have been directed toward improving the core French curriculum in English language schools. This interest and efforts have resulted in a concerted effort to expose all students to the French language in school and, where numbers warrant, to have students strengthen their first language. It is recognized that one's first language deserves to be encouraged and developed along the lines of two official languages. While these ideals have been clearly established, reality often falls short due to lack of financial resources and qualified personnel, especially in a large country with a dispersed population (Duquette, 1987).

Myths and misconceptions

At one time or another, most people have probably heard someone voice dire consequences about the results of multicultural education. Banks (1993), an acknowledged leader in the multicultural education movement, identifies and debunks several misconceptions about multicultural education.

Misconception 1 - Multicultural education is for others. Some people argue that multicultural education is an entitlement program and a curriculum movement for African Americans, Hispanics, the poor, women, and other victimized groups. Banks considers this belief to be a misconception. In fact, multicultural education as designed during the last decade, calls for a restructuring of educational institutions so that all learners will acquire the knowledge, skills, and attitudes needed to function effectively in a culturally diverse nation. Rather than focusing only on specific gender and ethnic movements, multicultural education tries to empower all students to become knowledgeable, caring, and active citizens (Banks, 1993).

Misconception 2 - Multicultural education is opposed to the Western tradition. Another harmful misconception about multicultural education has been the claim that the multicultural education movement opposes the West and Western civilization. Banks (1993) maintains that multicultural education is not anti-West, because many culturally diverse writers such as Rudolfo Anaya, Paula Gunn Allen, Maxine Hong Kingston, Maya Angelou, and Toni Morrison are Western writers. In fact, multicultural education is a thoroughly Western movement which grew out of the civil rights movement grounded in such democratic ideals as freedom, justice, and equality (Banks, 1993).

Misconception 3 - Multicultural education will divide the nation. Critics often claim multicultural education will divide the nation and undercut its unity. This misconception is based partly on questionable assumptions about the nature of U.S. society and partly on a mistaken understanding of multicultural education. The claim that multicultural education will divide the nation assumes an already united nation. Without doubt, the U.S. is one nation politically; however, sociologically our nation is deeply divided along lines of race, gender, and class. Multicultural education seeks to unify a deeply divided nation rather than to divide a highly cohesive one. Traditionally, U.S. society and the schools tried to create unity by assimilating students from diverse racial and ethnic groups into a mythical Anglo American culture that required a process of self-alienation. However, even when culturally diverse students became culturally assimilated, they continued to experience exclusion from the mainstream society (Banks, 1993).

Broad Goals in Promoting Multicultural Education

The goals for multicultural education programs listed earlier in the chapter pertained to K-12 programs. However, the uniqueness of young adolescents and the nature of middle school practices suggest the importance of multicultural education in middle level schools having a "young adolescent" focus and goals distinctly different from those of elementary and secondary schools. While one particular approach cannot be identified as being the most effective, one can safely state that whatever multicultural education program a middle level school may adopt, the nature, needs, and developmental characteristics of young adolescents must be primary considerations.

Goal 1 - Incorporate multicultural education to teach and instill respect for culturally diverse young adolescents and instill in them a respect for their cultural backgrounds, characteristics, and heritages.

Middle level schools and society as a whole benefit when young adolescents receive multicultural education experiences which instill respect for differences, both their own and in others. Developing at a crucial age, young adolescents form opinions of self and others which may last a lifetime. Effective multicultural education programs emphasize how differences enrich society, the importance of young adolescents developing feelings of acceptance, and the advantages of harmony among cultural groups. Likewise, regardless of cultural, ethnic, social class, generational, and other differences, it is imperative that young adolescents develop an appreciation for their cultural backgrounds, characteristics, and heritages. Youngsters living and coping in school environments different from their cultural backgrounds need to feel accepted and to have positive feelings about their culture rather than developing questions and concerns about the worthiness of their backgrounds.

Progress can be made toward such a goal when middle level educators provide accurate and objective knowledge of cultures, model genuine concern for promoting cultural diversity, and encourage others to accept others' differences.

Goal 2 - Provide curricular, organizational, instructional, and environmental approaches which reflect the cultural diversity of the students.

As mentioned previously and discussed in more detail in Chapters 3 and 4, making curricular, instructional, and environmental approaches reflect cultural diversity represents a major step toward promoting respect for cultural diversity. Rather than the multicultural education program being a fragmented effort or being more rhetoric than action, effective efforts are comprehensive. Curricular efforts include subject area content; accurate representations of culturally diverse people; multicultural art, music, and dance; and integrated curricular themes showing a recognition of cultural diversity. Instructional practices include considerations of culturally diverse young adolescents' perceptions of success; their motivational habits; and how they learn. Environmental factors include the degree of positive references to cultural diversity, emphasis on self-esteem and the promotion of cultural identities, and demonstration of respect and trust.

Perceptive educators recognize teaching as involving more than creating curriculum designs and engaging in classroom interaction. All classrooms function as social environments with several common dimensions: relationships among learners and teachers; the overall classroom climate; the assigning of tasks; and managerial rules and regulations. Working together, these dimensions form the social context and stage setting for learning (Gay, 1992).

Goal 3 - Promote self-esteem, cultural identities, and overall personal and social development of young adolescents.

Middle level educators readily understand the importance of positive self-esteem on learning and overall development. Perhaps not as fully understood, the development of a positive cultural identity is equally important, especially during these crucial developmental years. Individuals base their cultural identity upon a number of traits and values related to national or ethnic origin, family, religion, gender, age, occupation, socioeconomic level, language, geographical region, and exceptionality (Gollnick & Chinn, 1990). The identity is determined to a large degree by the interaction among these factors, and the degree to which individuals identify with different subcultures or cultural groups that share social and political institutions, and other distinctive cultural elements (Hernandez, 1989).

Santrock (1990) shows how others affect one's feelings toward oneself and the culture:

> The Hopi Indians are a quiet, thoughtful people, who go to great lengths not to offend anyone. In a pueblo north of Albuquerque, a 12-year boy speaks: "I've been living in Albuquerque for a year. The Anglos I've met, they're different. I don't know why. In school, I drew a picture of my father's horse. One of the other kids wouldn't believe that it was ours. He said, "You don't really own that horse." I said, "It is a horse my father rides, and I feed it every morning." He said, "I can ride a horse better than you, and I'd rather be a pilot." I told him I never thought of being a pilot.
>
> The 12-year-old Indian boy continues, "Anglo kids, they won't let you get away with anything. Tell them something, and as fast as lightning and as loud as thunder, they'll say, "I'm better than you are, so there!" My father says it's always been like that" (p. 382).

As our society and its schools continue to grow in diversity, middle level educators, working with young adolescents whose self-esteems and cultural identities change daily, will be challenged to help each young adolescent develop positive self-esteem and a cultural identity. Rather than allowing "different is wrong" perceptions to prevail, and to lower learners' opinions of their cultural identities, perceptive educators recognize learners' cultural identities and assist learners in developing positive, healthy identities. Teachers can take appropriate action to improve culturally diverse learners' opinions of their culture by: providing positive images of all people, regardless of race, culture, ethnic backgrounds, or social class; teaching about the contributions of all groups; ensuring equal and fair treatment for all learners and their families; and celebrating cultural diversity through appropriate multicultural educational experiences for all students.

Goal 4 - Ensure all middle level educators have the knowledge, awareness, and skills to work effectively in multicultural situations.

Effective classroom teachers, support service specialists, and administrators at both the school and district level accept responsibility for acquiring the knowledge, awareness, and skills necessary to be effective in multicultural classrooms. They understand the effects of culture on motivation, learning, and perceptions of success.

Through first-hand contact, journals, books, inservice work, coursework, and other sources of information, professional decisions regarding a learner's family, language, and unique problems can be reached with a degree of accuracy and objectivity. Knowledge, awarenes, and skills, however, require motivation on the educator's part and effective leadership both at the school and district level.

Goal 5 - Take deliberate action to lessen ethnocentrism, racist acts, stereotypical beliefs, and crimes of hate.

Chapter 1 pointed out the negative effects of these conditions. While these evils affect all learners and all society, young adolescents are especially affected. They need positive references to their individuality and cultural backgrounds rather than being the victims of injustice and stereotypical beliefs.

Young adolescents attending schools both in areas where these evils are commonplace occurrences and where they are more subtle and covert, benefit when their schools adopt a specific agenda focusing on cultural diversity and form a deliberate plan to curb violence. Maintaining a constant surveillance to detect any condition which can create distrust, injustice, and fear should be an integral component of this deliberate action.

Institutional racism, another insidious form of racism, hurts a learner's self-esteem, cultural identity, psychosocial development, and academic progress. Although such issues as equal opportunity, segregation, and inequities in educational opportunity have been vocalized and brought to the nation's attention during the past several decades, institutional racism often continues and results from otherwise well-meaning efforts. Some believe that the society has done away with racism through legislation and special programs; however, realistically speaking, some school practices continue to have negative effects such as tracking, segregation due to presumed ability, and stereotypical expectations for achievement and behavior (Pine & Hilliard, 1990). The reduction and ultimate elimination of overt and institutional racism must be addressed by middle level schools.

Similarities of Multicultural Education and the Middle School Concept

The multicultural education movement and the middle school concept share several notable similarities. Both movements grew in popularity during the latter half of the 21st century and both reflect and complement each other in at least two distinct ways.

Student-centered philosophies and actions

First, both multicultural education and the middle school movement reflect student-centered philosophies and actions. Multiculturalism espouses the dignity and worth of all students. Similarly, the middle school movement espouses a strong belief in helping, nurturing, promoting, and respecting individual learners. Middle level educators' concern and respect for individuals also includes acceptance of the same differences prescribed by multicultural education doctrines. The focus of both movements is on the individual.

Respecting diversity of all forms

Second, both the multicultural education movement and the middle school movement demonstrate the importance of respecting diversity of all forms. Multicultural education is strongly committed to recognizing positively cultural, ethnic, gender, and social class differences. The middle level education movement, likewise, offers a sincere commitment to young adolescents' varying physical, psychosocial, and intellectual characteristics and responds to their cultural diversity. For example, middle school perspectives espoused in *This We Believe* (National Middle School Association, 1992) takes the position that young adolescents' widely differing developmental characteristics as well as cultural and ethnic backgrounds should be reflected in teaching and learning experiences.

Early Adolescence—A Crucial Time for Multicultural Education

Several aspects of early adolescence contribute to its being a critical time to provide developmentally appropriate multicultural education experiences. Young adolescents' psychosocial and intellectual developmental characteristics allow self-examination, the forming of mindsets of others and their diversity, and forming opinions toward concepts crucial to the welfare of individuals and our society such as justice, equality, and acceptance. This section examines how effective multicultural education programs can help young adolescents form positive opinions of others and their own cultural backgrounds.

Young adolescents form self-esteem and a cultural identity which may last a lifetime.

Middle level educators face significant challenges daily because the 10-14 year old developmental period is crucial for self-esteem development and identity formation (Manning & Allen, 1987). Young adolescents' perceptions of cultural differences and their opinions of others' perceptions play significant roles in their degree of self-worth. For example, a student culturally different from the teacher and coming from a lower socioeconomic level may, indeed, understandably consider "differences" as inferior or wrong. Perceptive educators recognize the disastrous consequences such feelings can have on young adolescents' sense of personal worth.

Special steps such as the following two can be taken to promote positive self-esteem and cultural identities.

1. Educators, through advisory and exploratory programs and the academic core, can help majority-culture and culturally diverse learners understand "culture," recognize how it affects peoples' lives, and understand that values cannot readily be placed upon culture.

2. Educators can work toward providing all young adolescents with accurate and objective materials and lead discussions of culture and cultural differences that clarify as many myths, distortions, and stereotypes as possible.

Young adolescents form opinions of others, both culturally diverse and majority culture.

The individual's needs for belonging and acceptance increase during the transition from childhood to adolescence. An educational environment that provides appropriate multicultural education experiences contributes to development of worthy cultural identities, positive self-esteem, and the formation of positive opinions of others. Middle level educators can help young adolescents form positive opinions of others in several ways such as the following four examples:

1. Since young adolescents usually choose friends with characteristics and traits similar to their own, encourage young adolescents to realize that traits and characteristics they want in a friend may be found in students of all cultures.

2. Encourage young adolescents to look beyond skin color when selecting friends, members of a cooperative learning team, and in other situations where educators expect students to "team-up" with other students.

3. Emphasize the absolute necessity of looking beyond stereotyping, myths, and misperceptions when forming opinions of others.

4. Model respect and acceptance of others, both young adolescents in the class and other professionals in the school.

Young adolescents form close friendships and social networks.

Making friends is important to young adolescents. Living and learning in multicultural schools and neighborhoods, they often know culturally different boys and girls who are potential friends, yet too often form friendships exclusively along racial lines due to either racism, stereotypical perceptions, or the belief that race is the most significant determining factor when selecting friends. Perceptive educators can take corrective action in several directions.

1. Teach that differences are not "right" or "wrong" and the decision to make friends should not be based on culture-based conditions.

2. Encourage cross-cultural study groups, cooperative learning groups, or peer-tutoring sessions so young adolescents can work together. While this intervention provides opportunities for socialization and for making friends, the teacher does not "make" friends or force "potential friends" to work together.

3. Understand the changing nature of friendships and be concerned but not alarmed if a class appears to be separated by cultures. Cross-cultural friendships can still occur over time, especially when the teacher plans teaching-learning experiences requiring interaction among young adolescents of all cultures.

Young adolescents' psychosocial and cognitive development contributes to their developing a sense of justice, a perception of fairness, and an overall sense of how people should be treated.

Teaching young adolescents who are concerned with justice, fairness, and poor treatment of others can be a challenging and rewarding experience. Young adolescents' developmental period contributes to their sense of fairplay and justice at the same time that their socialization increases, others are being considered as possible friends, and opinions of diversity are being formed. They often voice concerns about the fairness of situations, about the injustices received by a group of people, or perhaps, sometimes the ill treatment teachers and parents inflict upon young people. Middle level educators can take advantage of young adolescents' developing senses of justice and fairplay.

1. Discuss in advisor-advisee sessions perceived situations in the school and community.

2. Provide exploratory experiences which emphasize the ill effects of racism and discrimination.

3. Emphasize in curricular areas, particularly social studies and literature, situations in which people have been treated unfairly and the ill effects of such treatment.

Young adolescents are becoming capable of engaging in social analysis, making judgments regarding personal and social behaviors, and developing a sense of morality and ethical behavior.

Since some young adolescents might still be thinking in concrete terms while others have advanced to abstract thought, it is imperative that they be considered as individuals. Those who are abstract thinkers can participate in social analysis of how and why people treat others as they do, form a basis for their own judgments, and think through ethical and moral situations. The three processes correspond closely with how young adolescents perceive racism, bias, and unjust treatment. Teaching young adolescents the effects of racism, discrimination, and unjust treatment of individuals has the potential for influencing learners' analysis of social situations and for influencing learners' developing sense of moral and ethical behavior.

Educators helping young adolescents with these processes can take several directions. First, home-based guidance activities or the counselor can provide activities which help young adolescents better understand their behavior and the reasons for acting as they do. Second, exploratory activities can encourage learners to read developmentally-appropriate books, carefully selected to show the effects of unjust treatment of others. Third, educational experiences can include exercises that help learners to understand how morality and ethical behavior, either directly or indirectly, affect others. Activities may include plays, short skits, the writing of dialogue based on a book such as *Sounder,* and role-playing which illustrates how people suffer from others' lack of caring or ill-considered behavior.

Summary

The multicultural education movement has flourished during the last two decades of the 20th century. Similarly, the movement to reform middle level education has been occurring during this same era. Fortunately, for young adolescents, the multicultural education movement and the middle level education movement both advocate respect for individuals and their differences. While multicultural education is important for learners of all grade levels, multicultural education is even more important for young adolescents whose psychosocial and intellectual development make early adolescence an ideal time to teach about differences among people and to teach concepts such as justice, democracy, and equality. The possibilities for young adolescents are nearly limitless when middle level educators plan educational experiences that reflect the cultural diversity of the school. ◆

3

Culturally Appropriate Middle Level Schools

Diversity is not a subtraction, it is an additive.

CHAPTER OUTLINE

Culturally Appropriate
Middle Level Schools

3

E ffective middle level educational experiences should reflect the multiculturalism of the United States. Young adolescents need a school program that fosters acceptance and appreciation for cultural diversity. Having one area of the middle school program reflect multiculturalism will not be sufficient. This chapter looks at essentials such as the need for comprehensive guidance and counseling programs, extensive exploratory programs, established communities of learning, appropriate organizational patterns, the involvement of parents and families, and the cultural composition of the faculty and staff. Multiculturalism should be integrated into all school functions so that cognitive and affective endeavors reflect multiculturalism, and the middle school functions as an example of how a diverse nation should operate. Such a learning environment necessitates examining all facets of the school day and all program components to determine whether the school honestly and genuinely reflects multiculturalism.

Prerequisites for a Successful Program

At least three conditions need to exist if a school is to conduct a successful multicultural program: (1) educators who genuinely are dedicated to promoting multiculturalism and bringing young adolescents into the mainstream of school activities and society; (2) a deliberate and comprehensive agenda for promoting multiculturalism; and (3) a commitment to provide all young adolescents with equal access to all educational programs and experiences.

Concern for and commitment to culturally diverse young adolescents

This prerequisite might appear simplistic, yet in some ways, it might be the most important factor in determining the school's success in providing multicultural teaching-learning experiences and environments. While many people speak favorably of all people and their differences, one does not have to look far to see racism and unjust acts. Victims are often blamed for their predicaments, i.e., students with reading problems often receive blame and condemnation, or the poor are blamed for their family's economic situation. Sometimes, educators blame learners due to misunderstandings rather than any outright prejudice. For example, Hispanic and Native American students have sometimes been considered lazy or not wanting to excel when, in actuality, the problem is these learners are being considered through a middle-class Anglo American perspective.

Many educators have dedicated themselves to removing even the most subtle forms of racist behavior in classrooms and have directed their efforts toward obtaining curricular materials free from bias. However, educators planning teaching and learning experiences need to avoid Pollyannish allusions that prejudice and bias no longer exist. Unquestionably, racism and non-acceptance of those in minority cultures continue to plague society as evidenced by increasing incidents of racism (Pine & Hilliard, 1990). Likewise, public recognition of these problems is growing; in a recent *New York Times*/CBS News poll (Racial division persists...., 1993), only 37 percent of Americans rated the nation's race relations as good.

Young adolescents need to feel that teachers respect differences and will treat them like majority culture learners. They should also feel that the middle school program contributes to their succeeding.

Total school commitment to multicultural educational approaches

All educators can recall educational innovations, pilot programs, and other endeavors offered in good faith that did not live up to expectations or result in instant success. Educators with enduring commitments to multicultural education will launch and stay with comprehensive efforts to meet the needs of culturally diverse learners.

For multiculturalism to become an integral aspect of the school, efforts must include all aspects of the school day: the curriculum, guidance activities, exploratory programs, social activities, teacher-student relationships, school rules, and other aspects of the school. A one-shot Multicultural Week or unit featuring African American history, tacos, and oriental dresses and customs will not suffice. While planned with the best intentions, anything less than total school commitment will not provide the long-term change needed, especially when as soon as the week of activities ends, the school routine returns to "business as usual." The curriculum, learning environment, and the mindset of learners, faculty, and staff members need to reflect multiculturalism as well as the cultural diversity of the school and nation (Manning, 1991).

Equal access—both philosophically and in practice

The concept of equal access holds that all learners should have equal opportunity to participate in educational experiences, learning programs, extracurricular activities, and teachers' attention. The gap between exclusivity and equal opportunity has narrowed somewhat during the last decade, predominantly in areas required by legal mandates. Unfortunately, some middle level schools, sometimes quite unknowingly, still fail to provide equal access to all educational experiences (Manning, 1993a).

School practices that deny equal access include:

- ability grouping in which lower-achieving youngsters often receive less than adequate curricular materials, the least interesting instructional methods, and sometimes the least qualified teachers;

- cheerleading competitions in which scores of girls and boys may try out but only a handful will be chosen;

- drama activities where only a few students are finally selected (one middle school had auditions for the school play and nearly a hundred students tried out for eleven parts, and even worse, the teachers only needed four girls); and

- students facing choices that deny, for instance, opportunities to participate in both art and band (Manning, 1993a).

Still other more subtle challenges exist to the equal access concept. While violations are not as blatant, sometimes African American boys and girls are "expected" to play basketball while Anglo-American students are guided to the tennis teams. Asian Americans are sometimes "expected" to participate only in the academic activities such as the science or mathematics clubs. While students may not be blatantly denied opportunities to participate, some may actually be "steered" in directions which educators think are most appropriate. Teachers, perhaps unconsciously, sometimes have higher expectations for boys than girls, for middle and higher social classes than for lower-classes, and for particular cultures. Inevitably, these expectations influence teaching methods and the commitment to helping all students succeed.

The concept of equal access deserves serious consideration. Equal access clearly affirmed in the schools' philosophy statements indicates that all students, regardless of cultural, gender, or social class, have equal access to all educational programs and school-sponsored experiences.

Culturally Appropriate Middle Level Practices

Recognizing the need to base middle level practices on learner differences

Learners perceive and learn about the world in different ways and demonstrate their understanding in different ways (Swisher, 1992). However, the organizational structure of the American school system, i.e., its grade levels, divisions within grades, and graded textbooks, contributes to educators expecting or assuming a great deal of homogeneity which, in fact, does not exist. A sixth or seventh grade teacher may begin to consider all twelve or thirteen year olds alike. Thornburg (1982) wrote over a decade ago that diversity was the hallmark characteristic of young adolescents. The increasing cultural diversity of our nation has extended this diversity. Middle level educators that recognize this provide teaching-learning experiences that reflect learning styles, perceptions of success, definitions of motivation, preferences to work cooperatively rather than competitively, and other differences. While learners have never been "alike," differences at the middle level are more pronounced than at other levels.

Classroom environments

Teaching in multicultural classrooms involves more than creating curriculum designs and engaging in classroom discourse. Other essential components include the physical, social, and intrapersonal climates in which learners work and socialize. Specific dimensions include relationships among students and teachers, climate conditions, task orientations, and managerial rules and regulations (Gay, 1992).

Students of some cultural groups find typical learning environments to be cold, formal, and disconcerting, often to an extent these conditions distract them from concentrating on academic tasks. Lining up to enter and exit the room, sitting in straight rows, and emphasis on individual competition are examples of such practices. Many culturally diverse learners prefer group arrangements; integration of affective, cognitive, and psychomotor responses; and active interaction of all environmental factors such as emotional factors and tones being considered (Gay, 1992).

Maintaining that the total school environment needs reforming, Banks (1987) offered several insights into creating appropriate school environments in our culturally diverse society:

1. Ethnic content should be incorporated into all subject areas in all grades.

2. Ethnic diversity should be reflected in learning centers, libraries, and resource centers, i.e., resources on history, literature, music, folklore, views of life, and the arts of the various groups of people.

3. Ethnic diversity should be reflected in assembly programs, classrooms,

hallway and entrance decorations, cafeteria menus, counseling interactions, and extracurricular activities.

4. Ethnic diversity should be reflected in school-sponsored dances and other school activities.

Ability grouping—effects on culturally diverse learners and alternatives

Research on ability grouping has provided enough evidence on its devastating effects to justify educators eliminating the practice altogether (George & Alexander, 1993; George, 1993; Manning & Lucking, 1990; Wheelock, 1993). The case against ability grouping has been forcefully made: ability grouping does not enhance academic achievement; it lowers the self-esteem of learners in lower ability groups; teachers use less effective instructional behaviors with the lower groups; and it teaches implicitly that some persons are worth more than others. In fact, evidence for over a half century has questioned its effectiveness and pointed out its negative consequences (Purdom, 1929).

The negative effects on culturally diverse learners are especially severe. Culturally diverse learners tend to receive placements in lower ability groups, perhaps due to lack of previous educational opportunities, or in some cases, simply because of stereotypical practices. The likelihood of ability grouping resulting in a form of segregation warrants educators' attention and concern. Ability grouping patterns often parallel students' nonacademic characteristics such as race or ethnic background, socioeconomic status, or personal appearance. Students from lower socioeconomic status and minority families are most often placed in lower ability groups. Such practices may be discriminatory because students are segregated along ethnic and social class lines (Dawson, 1987).

Regardless of the reason, for many culturally diverse learners, the results are the same: Culturally diverse learners develop low self-esteem and perhaps question their cultural worth. Some learners do not get the educational experiences they need, i.e., second language training, and some are subjected to less effective instructional methods. A serious problem arises when learners feel like second-rate citizens and are denied the opportunities necessary for educational success.

Educators should select organizational patterns which either eliminate or reduce the negative consequences of ability grouping. Possibilities include the following:

1. Cooperative learning provides a set of alternatives to traditional instruction systems in which students work in heterogeneous groups of four to six members and earn recognition, rewards, and sometimes grades based on the academic achievement of their groups (Slavin, 1983). (A more detailed discussion of cooperative learning is provided in the next section).

2. Heterogeneous grouping wherein students are organized with a mixture of ability levels, ethnic groups, and socioeconomic levels and teachers adapt the learning environment to meet the needs of individuals or small groups.

3. The Joplin Plan which is actually a form of regrouping in which students are assigned to heterogeneous groups for the major portion of the school day and then regrouped for reading across grade levels (Slavin, 1987).

4. Individualization is probably the most effective means of instructing learners, but is difficult to do when faced with large numbers.

5. Mastery learning requires constantly changing teaching and learning decisions to reflect student performance, i.e., students take a test which determines whether they take enrichment activities or remedial work (Slavin, 1988). Achieving a predetermined level of mastery must occur before new work is taken up.

The evidence is stacked convincingly against ability grouping. Since young adolescents are forming the self-esteem that will last a lifetime and are forming perceptions of others that will determine their actions, working in classrooms segregated by culture or social class does not allow appropriate perceptions of others to develop. Nor does it allow cross-cultural friendships and opportunities to contribute to the racial harmony our nation desperately needs. Classrooms ought to be as representative of our nation's diversity as possible given the school district's population, especially since a full education includes much more than simply acquiring facts and figures.

Cooperative learning—cultural considerations

Research reveals cooperative learning contributes to improved interpersonal and multicultural relationships and to the improvement of culturally diverse learners' self-esteem, cultural identities, overall feelings of self-worth; and academic achievement (Manning & Lucking, 1993).

There are several reasons why cooperative learning is effective in multicultural classrooms. First, learners in integrated education settings working toward similar goals must communicate effectively with one another, understand the advantages associated with positive group dynamics, and recognize differences as enriching to classrooms They must recognize the value of helping others rather than working competitively. Additionally, culturally diverse learners' cultural characteristics often contribute to the dynamics involved with cooperative learning. For example, Little Soldier (1989) suggests that cooperative learning matches Native American values and behaviors such as respect for individuals' opinions and feelings, the development of an internal locus of control, and the promotion of cooperation, sharing, and harmony. Finally, the goals of cooperative learning contribute significantly to the processes which build, promote, and sustain positive interpersonal relationships among majority cultures and culturally diverse learners.

For example, the positive feelings toward learner differences required for success-ful cooperative learning compare favorably with the attitudes needed for positive intercultural relationships.

Much remains unknown about how racial attitudes develop and change, but positive human interaction among individuals of different races or cultures does contribute to harmonious feelings on the part of all. However, simply providing mere classroom interaction is probably not a sufficiently powerful force to change students' racial or cultural attitudes which have developed over periods of time. In fact, Slavin (1983), a prolific writer on cooperative learning, addressed this issue over a decade ago. In doing so, he cited the Allport Contact Theory of Interracial Relations (Allport, 1954), which holds that for individuals of different races to develop positive relationships, they must engage in frequent cooperative activity on an equal basis. In cooperative learning situations, culturally diverse students are assigned to groups and given an equal identity. They then work toward a common, shared goal and engage in effective communication which subsequently leads to mutually positive feelings.

Peer tutoring/peer advising

Dentzer and Wheelock (1990) suggested that, given limited opportunities for teachers to provide assistance, peer tutoring can be an effective teaching-learning tool. Without doubt, students working together to help other students, whether academically or socially, can learn from one another. Perceptive teachers can think of many opportunities for young adolescents to tutor others, both within the class and perhaps in other classes or even grades. Tutoring another student, both in the planning for and in the dialogue with the learner being tutored, provides an excel-lent means of clarifying one's understanding of a topic or concept.

Peer advising also can play a major role in the middle school. For example, a student who either has refused to succumb to peer pressure or who has experienced first hand the consequences of "going with the crowd" can be an excellent advisor to a student being pressured by peers. In fact, a student might be more receptive to a student advisor than to an adult. Likewise, knowledgeable and capable young adolescents might serve as advisors in such areas as peer pressure, tobacco, alcohol and drug abuse, sexuality, and equating personal wishes and parents' and teachers' expectations. Peer tutoring and advising play especially vital roles in multicultural settings. Several benefits can result when young adolescents tutor or advise in cross-cultural settings.

- Students learn more about cultural differences and realize that people are more alike than different.

- Students can benefit from individual attention that the teacher
    cannot provide.

- Students may be able to explain a concept or advise about a
    problem from a developmentally appropriate perspective.

- Students enjoy the feeling of helping others and working
    cooperatively.

- Students benefit from cross-cultural socialization.

The vast developmental differences in achievement levels which exist along with tremendous cultural differences challenge teachers' time and expertise. One partial answer to the challenge, peer tutoring and advising, can both contribute to academic learning and provide much-needed socialization opportunities for young adolescents.

Teacher advisory programs

Comprehensive guidance and counseling programs have been espoused as essential to the middle school concept in *This We Believe* (National Middle School Association, 1992). The advisor-advisee program, in particular, plays a vital role in the middle school (George & Alexander, 1993; James, 1986; Connors, 1992). This section examines advisor-advisee programs largely from a multicultural perspective.

A teacher advisory program can make notable contributions in multicultural settings. These small, intimate groups can provide improved communication between cultures; the recognition of problems which otherwise might have gone unnoticed; a better understanding of racism and the effects of discrimination; a heightened level of appreciation of cultural differences; an understanding of how different cultures consider friendships, peers, and allegiance to family expectations; as well as a realization of the dangers associated with stereotypes.

The advisees should suggest topics themselves, although allowing this does not mean the program would lack structure. A carefully planned agenda is needed for each advisor-advisee session; however, sufficient flexibility should allow a change of topics or allow a current event to take precedence over planned topics. For example, national, state, or local events involving racism, immigration, or any topic related to the cultural diversity of our nation can be discussed and clarified whenever they are current.

The fact that advisory programs can readily incorporate multiculturalism is "good in and of itself," but it also necessary to include multiculturalism in cognitive areas as well. The affective aspects of facts, topics, and events discussed in the various subject areas can be addressed in the advisory program, i.e., students studying the facts of discrimination in a social studies class can learn more about the personal effects in advisory settings as students share actual experiences with discrimination. In essence, the cognitive and affective areas complement one another when teachers carefully coordinate advisory sessions and topics.

Exploratory programs

This We Believe (National Middle School Association, 1992) called for middle schools to have full exploratory programs because young adolescents, by their nature, are explorers and adventurers. They should have opportunities to identify their interests, ascertain their aptitudes, and develop skills within personal and educational constructs. They must identify who and what they are and consider who and what they want to and can become (NASSP, 1993, p. 9). Appropriate exploratory programs should help young adolescents define and pursue their current living and learning needs and consider how their developing interests and capacities can influence future school and life decisions (NASSP, 1993).

Exploratory and enrichment opportunities may include an extension of any specific academic interest; arts and crafts, theatrical and musical performing experiences; games and physical activities; independent study opportunities; personal improvement programs; and clubs and student organizations.

Among the procedures teachers can use for establishing student-centered exploratory experiences are the following:

- young adolescents in consultation with their teachers can identify and carry out exploratory opportunities which are personally interesting and intellectually stimulating;

- firsthand experiences in the school or community can be organized;

- exploratory classroom activities based on learners' experiences can be conducted; and

- learners can assume the responsibility for organizing their experiences and sharing their observations with other students (Allen, Splittgerber, & Manning, 1993).

Exploratory activities which reflect multiculturalism include topics in four broad areas: (1) allowing young adolescents to learn more about their own cultural heritages; (2) understanding others' cultural backgrounds; (3) viewing differences as positive rather than negative; and (4) recognizing the need for cooperation and harmony. Appropriate topics may include:

- examining a culture's history, traditions, customs, and families;

- exploring the challenges facing culturally diverse people today;

- studying art, dance, and/or music of a particular culture;

- studying successful people (scholars, scientists, writers, artists, musicians) in a particular culture; and

- reviewing past immigration patterns and America's current reactions to the recent flood of immigrants.

Exploratory programs play a special role in multicultural education programs because they provide young adolescents opportunities to explore areas of interest and because various multicultural topics are certain to be included. Equally important, both majority and culturally diverse students, can, within limits, choose their own exploratories. Independent study arrangements can make it possible for students to select topics related to their culture or others' culture and with the teachers' help, plan an individual exploratory experience. Multiculturalism needs to permeate all aspects of an exploratory program. Focusing only on middle class Anglo perspectives fails to demonstrate a serious commitment to multicultural education.

Since this section only examines exploratory programs from multicultural perspectives, readers wanting a more detailed discussion of exploratory programs are referred to *Exploration: The Total Curriculum*, by Compton and Hawn (1993).

Communities of learners

Young adolescents often feel anonymous after transferring from an elementary school to a larger middle school. These feelings of being alone or unknown may be even more widespread with culturally diverse learners. The advantages of the "communities of learning" concept extend to both cognitive and psychosocial development. Learners working in small teams get to know one another sufficiently to create a climate for both socialization and cognitive development while reducing the discontinuity in expectations and practices among teachers, the separateness of subject areas, and the instability of peer groups. Every young adolescent ought to have at least one thoughtful adult who has the time and initiative to talk about personal problems, academic affairs, and the importance of having positive feelings about oneself and one's school. Culturally diverse learners especially need to be a part of a community of learners. Opportunities for both academic learning and socialization reduce feelings of anonymity, make learners feel known or a part of the class activities, and demonstrate to young adolescents that teachers care about culturally diverse learners and consider them significant and accepted members of the class.

If young adolescents have not previously worked or socialized together, preparation to work cooperatively with others should provide for:

- explaining to both the majority culture and culturally diverse learners the concept of and purposes of "communities of learning";

- comparing this concept to our democratic society and clarifying the similarities;

- explaining how cultural perceptions may differ yet not be wrong, i.e., perceptions of success, and working cooperatively rather than competitively; and

- teaching participants to fulfill roles and be both good leaders and followers.

As with other middle school practices, efforts need to focus on determining whether all young adolescents are accepted members of the community and whether academic and social goals are being met. Questions such as the following should be examined: Are all students integral and working members of the community? Are "communities of learning" representative of our society or are they segregated by race, culture, or social class? Do "communities of learning" help learners feel a part of school and society?

Academic counseling

Academic counseling provides young adolescents access to critical information about the curriculum and its implications for career and later schooling. Successful academic counseling also provides continuous, effective communication between teachers and counselors so that students receive timely, accurate, and specific communication. Students need a clear concept of their cognitive ability presented in such a way that self-esteem does not suffer. During these years, young adolescents develop lifelong values and attitudes about the significance of education and about their chances of succeeding in upwardly mobile academic and career choices. A strong academic counseling program also includes direct, substantive parent involvement, so parents can offer input and different perspectives as well as be aware of academic options and career choices (California State Department of Education, 1987).

Academic counseling can be particularly beneficial to culturally diverse learners. First, some first and second generation learners and their parents might not understand the American school system and especially the role of the middle school. Second, some culturally diverse learners may experience academic problems due to language limitations, other communication problems (such as nonverbal communication), and perhaps teachers' stereotypical misperceptions. Third, while not the culturally diverse learners' fault, sometimes middle class Anglo American teachers' opinions of success, competition, and motivation differ from culturally diverse learners' opinions. Academic counselors might need to address both opinions and show learners that differing opinions do not imply right or wrong. Fourth, culturally diverse learners sometimes do not know options available to address their particular strengths and weaknesses. Counseling can include helping culturally diverse young adolescents have access to needed programs, remedial, enrichment, and otherwise. It is important to note, however, that this ought not include the use of tracking or ability grouping.

Counselors may need to enhance their knowledge of culturally diverse populations, sharpen their skills to work effectively with these young adolescents, and reexamine their attitudes toward diversity. Counselors need to understand culturally diverse learners' outlooks on life, perceptions of schools and teachers, opinions of success, motivation, and competition, and special challenges which culturally diverse learners face in American schools. Gaining needed knowledge and skills can be accomplished through coursework, seminars, inservice work, conferences, reading appropriate journals and books, and, of course, firsthand experiences with culturally diverse young adolescents.

Developmental Issues: Middle Level Schools Reflecting Cultural Differences

Lipsitz (1984) found that the most striking feature of successful schools was their willingness to adapt all school practices to the individual differences in cognitive, biological, and social maturation of their students. The schools began "from the beginning to be positive environments for early adolescent personal and social development, not only because such environments contribute to academic development, but because they are intrinsically valued, stemming from a belief in positive school climate as a goal, not a process toward a goal" (p. 168).

This section examines development and cultural differences. Just as differences (developmental and other) exist between Anglo Americans, differences also exist between and among culturally diverse groups.

Possibilities, hurdles, and questions

Any reasonable discussion of development among culturally diverse learners must acknowledge a possibility and a hurdle. First, the possibility exists that research conducted on middle class Anglo American learners might not apply to culturally diverse learners. For example, Werner (1979) in her *Cross-Cultural Child Development: A View From the Planet Earth,* concluded several factors affected development: acculturation, the degree of Western-type schooling, ecological-economic demands, maternal styles, socialization, values, and sex differences. Werner's work causes one to question whether conclusions regarding culturally diverse learners can be formed with any significant degree of certainty. Second, a hurdle poses another challenge to middle school educators. Until recently, very little work focused on the development of culturally diverse young adolescents. Development studies focused almost exclusively on children and adolescents. One breakthrough, *Child Development* (April 1990), devoted an issue to minority children and much of our present knowledge of culturally diverse young adolescents comes from that issue. Likewise, in the past decade, the *Journal of Early Adolescence* has published articles on culturally diverse young adolescents. Werner (1979) reported the largest number of studies focusing on children's passages from Piaget's preoperational stage (2-7 years) to the concrete operational stage. Likewise, Tucker and Huerta (1987) studied developmental tasks in young adult Mexican American females (ages 18-34) and concluded that these women experienced the developmental tasks suggested by Havighurst (1972).

The limited research on culturally diverse young adolescents does not mean middle level educators should ignore development. Quite the contrary, all middle level experiences should have a developmental basis; however, caution should be exercised when drawing definitive conclusions.

Friendships and social networks

Research on friendships and social networks indicates making friends might be more complicated due to the steadily increasing cultural diversity of the U.S. (Deegan, 1992); in both school and out-of-school contexts more young adolescents develop their own race choices rather than other race choices; and African Americans are twice as likely as Anglo Americans to see other race school friends outside of school (DuBois & Hirsch, 1990).

Realizing the importance of friendships to the psychosocial development of young adolescents, middle school educators can take several steps: first, by modeling behaviors contributing to friendships and overall social development; second, by providing opportunities for socialization and the making of friends, through peer tutoring, cooperative learning, and other small group work while maintaining a heterogeneously grouped classroom; and third, by promoting cross-culture friendships.

Special attention should be given to the homeless, social isolates, loners, the friendless, and individuals who are the victims of jokes and cruelty resulting from racial slurs, personal appearance, or handicaps. Such cruelties take a serious toll on young adolescents during these developmental years. These young people need friends, and while educators cannot "make" friends for those who lack friends, they can include these learners in social activities and assist them in becoming more socially acceptable.

Quests for freedom and independence

Anyone acquainted with young adolescents knows of their quest for freedom and independence. From choosing their own clothes to selecting book covers, they want control of their lives and behaviors. Parents and teachers are often upset by young adolescents participating in previously unheard of behaviors, questioning home and school rules, and appearing brave and challenging. When many young adolescents demonstrate such behaviors, educators may begin to expect this overt quest for freedom and independence from all.

While seeking independence may be a developmental characteristic of young adolescents, extreme behaviors should not be expected of all young adolescents, especially culturally diverse learners. Native Americans, for instance, according to existing beliefs, are less assertive and adhere more to tribal and family expectations. Asian Americans have a powerful allegiance to the family, both immediate and extended, and avoid behaviors which might bring shame or dishonor on the family. Individual, cultural, social class, and generational differences, of course, affect all these behaviors; therefore, exceptions will also exist.

Appropriate guidelines for middle level educators include: (1) recognize that seeking freedom and independence is a natural characteristic of this developmental period; (2) recognize differences and respond appropriately rather than expecting all young adolescents to demonstrate the same behaviors; (3) recognize quests for freedom and independence may be expected and appreciated in the middle class Anglo American culture while other cultures may not value these behaviors and will misunderstand educators encouraging these behaviors; and (4) remember the diversity among individuals and cultures and treat all young adolescents as individuals.

Critical self-examination

Looking in the mirror, examining one's height and weight, considering one's athletic finesse, and generally speaking, comparing oneself with others are all common behaviors of young adolescents. They want to know how they "size-up" with peers and often base self-esteem on these traits. Minor imperfections are often blown out of proportion and greatly influence one's confidence to handle everyday situations. Middle level teachers and counselors recognize this critical self-examination, understand it is common, and try to help young adolescents be realistic in their self-appraisals.

Culturally diverse young adolescents may be at increased risk because many attend schools in which majority-culture expectations and standards receive respect. For example, opinions of how girls and boys should act and behave, fashionable clothing, particular bookbags, and perspectives toward success and competition might confuse or make little sense to culturally diverse learners, and subsequently, cause them to question their personal and cultural values. Educators need to help culturally diverse young adolescents understand that body size, facial appearance, hair color and type are not a matter of right and wrong and, therefore, one's self-evaluation should not be based upon other cultures' standards and expectations.

Self-esteem and cultural identities

Educators are acutely aware of the importance of middle schoolers developing a healthy self-esteem and, as the U.S. society grows more diverse, are rapidly recognizing the absolute necessity of young adolescents developing a positive cultural identity. The degree of worth 10-15 year olds attach to their self-esteem and cultural identity will greatly influence these formative years, and in many ways, the rest of their lives.

Phinney (1989) studied the development of Asian, African, Mexican, and Anglo American students' cultural identities and arrived at the following conclusions:

1. Culturally diverse learners experience a need to deal with their ethnicity in a predominantly Anglo American society.

2. Anglo American students generally do not recognize any ethnicity except being American;

3. Asian American students often demonstrate negative attitudes about themselves even though a generally positive view of Asians prevails in society.

4. Asian American students had trouble naming leading Asian role models, probably because of the lack of a social movement stressing ethnic pride which African and Mexican Americans have experienced.

The works of Purkey and Novak (1984) in *Inviting School Success* and Beane and Lipka (1987) in *When the Kids Come First: Enhancing Self-Esteem* have indicated the dire need to address learners' self-esteem and have suggested methods to raise feelings of self-worth. While neither of these works focused directly on culturally diverse learners, educators in multicultural situations can use many of the same techniques. Middle school educators can focus attention on helping culturally diverse young adolescents develop positive cultural identities. Culturally diverse young adolescents should be made aware of the positives of all cultures such as major contributions made by members of various cultures.

Sex role identification

Although some sex role identification occurs in the early years, young adolescents more completely define appropriate role behaviors for boys and girls. Once again it needs to be recognized that young adolescents in multicultural school settings may experience more difficulties and confusion, because sex role behaviors acceptable in one society might be unacceptable in another. Consider the following findings.

1. African Americans de-emphasize rigid sex roles, i.e. both men and women often assume household responsibilities, care for children, and work outside the home (Smith, 1981).

2. Asian Americans, particularly Chinese Americans, teach the father is patriarchal; the son's obligations to be a good husband and father come second to his duty as a son; females accept subservient roles, serve as childbearer and nurturing caretaker, and assume responsibility for domestic chores (Sue, 1981).

3. Hispanic Americans, i.e., in the Latino American family, the father is clearly the head of the household, children learn early the father's authority goes unchallenged, male dominance extends to sons, and daughters accept subservient roles (Lum, 1986). (It is important to note that Hispanic sex roles are being challenged and in some cases being redefined.)

4. Native Americans adhere to fairly specific sex roles. Traditionally, men and boys brought physical strength, while women and girls worked in the home and cared for children and the elderly (Attneave, 1982).

Rather than trying to persuade culturally diverse learners to adopt middle class Anglo American sex role perspectives, educators need to recognize the confusion culturally diverse learners might face and help them adapt their sex role behaviors with their culture and personal beliefs. Considerable caution must be taken to avoid the notion that middle-class Anglo American sex role behaviors are right and, therefore, all others are wrong.

Evaluation and psychological testing—cultural perspectives

In the 1970s, educators faced numerous legislative requirements for testing that reflected the concerns of the accountability movement. Legislators, believing schooling to be ineffective, mandated tests to show whether students could demonstrate at least minimal competence in the three R's (Popham, 1993). Young adolescents, and especially culturally diverse learners, are particularly vulnerable. They have left the safe elementary school and are experiencing rapid developmental changes, and for culturally diverse learners, are living and learning in a majority culture society. The Association for Childhood Education International has taken a strong stand against standardized testing in the early grades and called for testing in the remainder of the elementary years to be seriously reconsidered (Perrone, 1991). This concern also holds true for the middle grades. An overemphasis on testing can have negative effects on young adolescents' self-esteem, their developing cultural identities, and other developmental aspects.

Evaluation and testing should always be conducted with care because the process can effects learners' stress, create confusion about the purposes, and even lead to sleepless nights and nervous problems. The process might have more severe effects on culturally diverse learners who might be new to the intense testing many states administer, might not realize the need to demonstrate what they actually know, and might fail to see the rationale of such ratings and percentiles.

Psychological testing could pose an even greater risk for culturally diverse youngsters who are often assessed and labeled incorrectly by tests designed for mainstream students. Furthermore, standardized tests do not provide objective information about atypical students. The cultural environment also affects characteristics such as motivation, anxiety, interpersonal relationships, and familiarity with objective methods of testing (Samuda & Lewis, 1992). Psychological testing includes interpretation, observing, testing, and analyzing data. Three important questions warrant consideration:

1. Are psychological constructs or concepts universally valid?
2. Which tests are most culturally valid and why?
3. What ethical and legal responsibilities surround multicultural assessment?

Lonner and Ibrahim (1989) maintained that without appropriate assessment strategies, professionals are unable to diagnose problems, unable to develop appropriate goals, and unable to assess the outcomes of testing. Such a situation challenges professionals to understand the learner's cultural and social class background and to use combinations of testing approaches for accurate and objective evaluation results.

Since tests can have negative effects on all learners, testing in multicultural settings calls for focusing efforts in several directions.

1. Monitor effects of testing closely to determine whether culturally diverse learners experience undue stress or confusion with directions, perhaps resulting from second-language problems.

2. Explain testing purposes and procedures to both culturally diverse young adolescents and their parents and families and help them understand how test results will be used.

3. Work to reduce the stress and ill effects resulting from the testing process.

4. Be sure psychological tests recognize cultural diversity and reflect learners' values and perspectives.

Cultural perceptions of motivation and success

Most educators probably base perspectives of motivation and success on traditional mindsets. For example, the success story usually features the high achiever, the athlete who excels, or the strong, independent leader. These learners have "done something" with their potential or through powerful motivation have made notable accomplishments without extraordinary ability. These learners usually capture the respect of others.

These perspectives of motivation and success may not be compatible with many culturally diverse learners' perspectives. Hispanic American learners may not demonstrate motivation or success-oriented behaviors because they might not want to excel or stand-out among their peers. Likewise, Native Americans might appear reluctant to participate in classroom discussions and might prefer harmony over any disharmonious actions which might result from competition. Likewise, maintaining harmony with one's friends might be considered more of a success than excelling in academic pursuits. Asian Americans might not raise their hands during questioning because of their quiet demeanor. Schools and our nation place emphasis on independence and the ability to make decisions and take appropriate action, whereas Asian Americans often place emphasis on opinions of parents and the elderly who are thought to have great wisdom. Rather than making quick decisions, Asian Americans might want to consult elders for advice.

Administrator/Faculty/Staff Composition

While multicultural education programs may have lofty goals statements, perhaps one of the most effective measures of a school's commitment to cultural diversity can be seen in the actual cultural, ethnic, racial, and gender composition of administrators, faculty, and staff. Specifically, do school personnel reflect the cultural diversity of the student population or the community at large? If school personnel are predominantly from one background, one might justifiably ask whether the goals of the multicultural education programs are being translated into actual practice. Culturally diverse learners who hear the rhetoric of multiculturalism, but see members of culturally diverse groups only in custodial or menial positions, might begin to question the school's commitment to equal opportunity (Baruth & Manning, 1992). At the same time, it has to be recognized that there is a serious and widespread shortage of certified personnel among all minorities. Merely having a real commitment and widespread recruitment are rarely adequate.

Defending the goal of employing culturally diverse school personnel is, however, not difficult. Having diverse people on the staff demonstrates a commitment to include all people, regardless of background, and shows a respect for the legal mandates that seek to ensure equal opportunity. Deliberate recruitment efforts aimed at employing culturally diverse professionals should be ongoing.

Responsive multicultural education programs include a commitment by professionals at all levels to multiculturalism and an acceptance of all learners regardless of diversity. While classroom teachers might have the most direct influence because of their being in close proximity to learners, administrators have an indirect influence because of their responsibility for ensuring that multicultural education programs are implemented.

Having administrators, teachers, and support services personnel reflect the cultural diversity of the school, community, and nation is without doubt an honorable goal for all levels of schooling. However, achieving this goal is more important for middle level schools. Young adolescents' psychosocial and cognitive development allow them to consider previously unconsidered perspectives (such as the fairness of employing all Anglo American administrators and teachers in a fully integrated school), to consider concepts such as fairness, equality, and justice. Young adolescents can see the discrepancies between goal statements and actual practice, making them skeptical of schools' intentions. And culturally diverse learners seeing their culture represented only in maintenance staff and service workers can make them question their school's commitment as well as their cultural worth.

Culturally Diverse Parents and Families

The need for an objective consideration of individual learners and their backgrounds will continue to be an essential. Teachers often form basic expectations and judgments about children based upon stereotypical assumptions and others' opinions, and, subsequently, become powerful judges of students' abilities and, in some cases, a maker or breaker of learners' lives (Carew & Lightfoot, 1979).

Educators have long recognized the importance of involving families and gaining their support. However, adequately addressing culturally diverse families' needs has been the exception rather than the norm. Educators have generally focused attention on middle and upper class Anglo American parents. This section examines parents and families from a multicultural perspective and explains the need for educators' understanding of these families.

Understanding differences in culturally diverse parents and families

Educators often assume too much homogeneity among culturally diverse families rather than understanding the differences which distinguish one cultural group and family from another. First, intracultural and individual differences, educational backgrounds, acculturation, and urban and rural backgrounds all contribute to the diversity of families. Second, socioeconomic status and social class differences also contribute to differences in values, attitudes, behaviors, and beliefs. Teachers sometimes make stereotypical assumptions about the links between children's backgrounds and their overall school success (Carew & Lightfoot, 1979). For example, teachers often stereotype learners according to social class, e.g., the lower classes lack ambition. This constitutes a serious error and hints of classism or racism. Lower socioeconomic classes wanting to improve their status in life often meet with considerable frustration when faced with low education, high unemployment, other conditions associated with poverty, and the racism and discrimination all-too-often prevalent. Third, generational differences within a particular family result in varying beliefs and values and represent another obstacle to assuming homogeneity within a family. Older generations may be more prone to retaining old world values and traditions because of the tendency to live within close proximity to people of similar language, traditions, and customs (Osako & Liu, 1986).

Understanding the extended family concept

Educators also need to recognize the differences between Anglo American and culturally diverse families' beliefs toward the family. While Anglo Americans tend to demonstrate greater respect for immediate family members, culturally diverse families extend similar allegiance and respect to extended family members such as grandparents, aunts, uncles, cousins, older siblings, and unrelated adults (Lum, 1986). Instead of educators working with only the mother and father, more perceptive attempts include recognizing both immediate and extended families.

Understanding culturally diverse parents and families

Many still believe the old myth that poor parents living in depressed areas around inner-city schools do not care about their children's education. Believing the opposite, Lightfoot (1978) states "poor and minority parents expect that schools will support their child's entry into middle-class life" (p. 31), and minority families, regardless of social class, universally view education as the most promising means of attaining higher socioeconomic status.

Chavkin (1989) noted that teachers see culturally diverse parents not attending traditional school-parent activities and assume they do not care. They then give up trying to involve parents in educational efforts when, in fact, the problem is a misunderstanding of culturally diverse families' attitudes. Chavkin also pointed out that school staffs sometimes intimidate people unaccustomed to school policies and that they seldom invite culturally diverse families to participate in the planning of activities. In fact, one survey revealed 95% of culturally diverse parents indicated they wanted homework completed and they wanted to spend time helping their children get the best education (Chavkin, 1989).

Understanding culturally diverse families' attitudes and behaviors

While one would expect parents and teachers to be natural allies, Lightfoot (1978) suggested that families and schools often find themselves in great conflict with one another. This conflict can result from cultural misunderstandings, varying opinions of teacher and parent control, differing value systems, and confusion resulting from language differences. Regardless of the reason, culturally diverse parents may resist teachers' efforts to participate in the educational process. Educators have a responsibility to understand such reasons for resistance and to plan appropriate responses such as the following .

First, some family members may fear disclosing personal or familial matters which might reflect negatively on the family, the father's ability to manage home affairs, or parenting skills. To reveal difficulties with family members may arouse feelings of shame and the perception that one has failed the family (Hartman & Askounis, 1989).

Second, (and closely related to the above), some culturally diverse groups view the child's failure in either school achievement or behavior to be a negative reflection of their parenting skills. West (1983) tells the story of a teacher who felt that she was not reaching a Vietnamese student. Although he was not disruptive, he was not participating fully in class. When she requested a parent conference, the father came to school full of dismay, feeling that his son had done something terrible.

Third, resistance and discontinuities between families and schools become dysfunctional when they result from or reflect differences in power and status in the society. For example, when the origins of conflict result from inequality, ethnocentrism, or racism, culturally diverse parents and families feel excluded, powerless, and abused. When schools accentuate and reinforce inequalities and prejudices, learners do not receive viable and productive treatment. Instead, learners and their parents and extended families receive messages of ethnocentrism when socialization, acculturation, and learning provide only traditional perspectives of the dominant culture (Lightfoot, 1978).

Understanding communicational differences

Language differences between parents' language and the language spoken in the school can contribute to parents resisting educators' efforts. Examples include culturally diverse learners translating and explaining bulletins to parents sent home, and a mother who did not understand repeated notices written in English that her daughter did not attend school (Olsen, 1988). To lessen the problem associated with communication, both written and oral, one California school sent letters to parents in four languages and conducted meetings in six languages! The program also included encouraging parents to offer in native languages their responses and opinions about school services. Then the school translated their responses and reported back in parents' native languages (Davis, 1989).

Whether communicating by speaking directly, by telephoning, or by writing to parents, educators are responsible for not allowing language or communication differences, verbal or nonverbal, to interfere with overall communication. Several factors deserve attention. First, the parents' English might not allow effective communication. Second, nonverbal communication might pose a problem. The Anglo American who looks the Native American directly in the eye while communicating might be considered rude, while the educators might think the Native American glancing away to be a sign of disinterest or irritation. Another example of possible nonverbal problem would be when Asian American parents, who are especially sensitive to nonverbal messages, would construe a teacher's folded arms or other casual gestures as indicative of a indifferent attitude (Chavkin, 1989).

A telephone call from the teacher can be extremely threatening to culturally diverse parents, because they have come to expect bad news whenever the school calls. Marion (1979), writing specifically about calling culturally diverse parents, proposed the following guidelines for minimizing misunderstandings.

1. Address parents as Mr. or Ms. because culturally diverse parents often do not receive the same respect and courtesy as other people.

2. Use a tone of voice that clearly expresses respect and courtesy because a call from school usually raises anxiety levels.

3. Discuss the student's positive points prior to discussing the problem needing to be resolved.

4. Use language the parent understands, and in a tone that does not sound condescending.

5. Respond with empathy if the parent has difficulty understanding unfamiliar educational concepts (Marion, 1979).

Understanding the need to involve families as volunteers

The National School Volunteer Program cited several reasons for using parents as volunteers in the classroom and school: (1) relieving the professional staff of nonteaching duties; (2) providing needed services to individual learners to supplement classroom teachers' work; (3) enriching the experiences of children beyond those normally available in school; (4) building a better understanding of school problems among citizens, and (5) stimulating widespread citizen support for public education (Shea & Butler, 1985).

Culturally diverse parents and extended family members have numerous talents and skills to share with children and adolescents. However, culturally diverse groups often consider teachers as being authoritarian and worthy of honor. Therefore some culturally diverse people might be hesitant to "interfere" with school routines, or feel that their talents are not "worthy" to be shared with the school. The administrator's and the teacher's role in this situation is to encourage and convince people that schools are open to new ideas, and that their talents are worthy of sharing. Progress can be made toward this goal by sending home, at the beginning of the school year, a parent involvement questionnaire designed to determine skills, talents, and areas of expertise (Baruth & Manning, 1992).

Summary

In effort to improve the education of young adolescents, middle school experts usually address a number of essential aspects rather than narrowly focusing on one or two areas. In essence, the multicultural education movement adopted a similar path so significant changes could occur. The movement to include multiculturalism throughout the school day cannot be a half-hearted effort. Multicultural education needs to be a comprehensive approach which is reflected in the school curriculum, organizational structure, cultural composition of school personnel, as well as in middle school characteristics such as advisor-advisee and exploratory activities. Last, effective multicultural education programs include efforts to understand and include culturally diverse parents and families. Only when middle schools genuinely commit to a comprehensive approach will young adolescents have access to curricular experiences, instructional practices, and school environments which adequately celebrate multiculturalism. ◆

4

Culturally Appropriate
Multicultural School Curricula

Students enjoy the feeling of helping others and working cooperatively.

CHAPTER OUTLINE

Multicultural Curricula Reflecting U.S. Demographics - 89

Prerequisites - 91

Assessing curricula needs
Determining barriers to multicultural curricular experiences

A Proposed Curricular Model: Academic, Social, and Personal - 93

Defining curricular dimensions and incorporating multicultural perspectives
Academic
Social
Personal

Curricular Areas and Multiculturalism - 95

Individual subject areas: language arts, science, mathematics,
social studies, art, and music
Example of curricular unit reflecting multiculturalism
Selected books

An Integrated Curriculum - 104

An emerging curriculum vision
Integrated curriculum and multiculturalism
Themes, questions, and concerns
Teachers' roles

Essential Considerations for Curricula Reflecting Multiculturalism- 109

Developmentally appropriate
Middle level in nature
Culturally appropriate teaching-learning materials
Culturally appropriate teacher attitudes
Evaluating curricular efforts

Linguistically Different Learners: Issues and Teaching Strategies - 112

Problems with English
A controversial issue
Language and culture: inseparable relationships
Multicultural education programs emphasizing language diversity
Effective strategies for teaching linguistically different learners

Summary - 117

Culturally Appropriate
Multicultural School Curricula

4

The middle school movement during the first two or three decades of its existence understandably focused on organization and achieving consensus on the essentials of effective middle schools While this focus continues to be a major concern, the last few years have seen a greater concern with the middle school curriculum itself. What defines the middle school curriculum? What are the essential characteristics of a curriculum that meets the needs of young adolescents? How does the middle school curriculum differ from the elementary and secondary school curriculum? The National Middle School Association, James Beane (1991; 1992; 1993b), John Arnold (1991; 1994), and Chris Stevenson (1992), among others have taken a lead in instituting serious consideration of middle school curriculum.

Our nation's increased cultural diversity mandates that this curricular effort must include a major emphasis on providing young adolescents with a "culturally-rich curriculum" that reflects cultural diversity and teaches respect for cultural diversity. This chapter seeks to build upon the curriculum reform underway and is built on the premise that multiculturalism should permeate the middle school curriculum and reflect the changing demographics of the United States.

Multicultural Curricula Reflecting U.S. Demographics

Agreeing with the contention that the middle school movement has all but ignored the curriculum issue, Lounsbury (1991) wrote, "The reality is that American education has continued to give homage to a curriculum that was established in the last century under vastly different circumstances and for a markedly different clientele (p. 3)." This "markedly different clientele" includes the various culturally diverse groups addressed in Chapter 1. Traditionally, the middle school curriculum, like elementary and secondary curricula, has reflected a middle-class Anglo American perspective. Historical figures, cultural images, and perspectives toward historical events portrayed majority culture perspectives, probably because writers of textbooks and other curricula materials wrote to satisfy the needs of mainstream purchasers.

Planned and deliberate action should be taken to provide young adolescents with a curriculum that more nearly reflects the contributions of various cultural groups and recognizes the nature of a particular student body. Rather than focusing only on "famous" Anglo Americans, the curriculum can include biographical figures in other cultures. For example, while most students have heard of Native American warriors such as Sitting Bull or Cochise, many have not heard of Susan LaFlesche, the first female Native American to become a doctor of Western medicine, or Annie Dodge Wauneka, a Navajo woman whose accomplishments in helping her people combat tuberculosis won her the Presidential Medal of Freedom Award in 1963. Similarly, school curricula have not given equal treatment to such African American leaders as Rosa Parks, Benjamin Mays, and Thurgood Marshall, all of whom played critical roles in the Civil Rights struggle. Asian Americans, often ignored in curricular materials, include I.M. Pei, an architect, and Paul Chu, a superconductivity scientist. Last, young adolescents, especially those looking for role models, should have a curriculum which teaches about Caesar Chavez, Jose Pedro Greer, and Pauline Gomez, three Hispanic Americans who have contributed to both Hispanics and the nation as a whole.

Rather than perceiving the middle school curriculum as separate, discrete courses or subjects, contemporary thought (Beane, 1992; Beane, 1993a) views curriculum as needing to be integrated and reflecting all the experiences students encounter during the school day. This perspective is based upon the belief that while students learn from the various subject areas, they also learn from other aspects of the school day, i.e., teachers modeling respect for others; teachers understanding friendship patterns of culturally diverse groups and subsequently providing opportunities for students of various cultural backgrounds to work cooperatively; and teachers understanding self-esteem differences among culturally diverse learners and how self-esteem may be best addressed. Increased psychosocial and cognitive development allows young adolescents to distinguish between teachers' stated beliefs and everyday actions. For example, a teacher who teaches harmony among cultural groups yet allows segregated groups and subtly demonstrates stereotypical beliefs about culturally diverse learners teaches more with actions than with words. Also, teachers can provide curricular experiences that address culturally diverse students' learning styles and provide curriculum opportunities that address their friendship patterns, identity development, social expectations, and self-esteem.

Including culturally diverse figures and providing curricula experiences reflecting cultural differences are only representative examples of methods providing young adolescents with a curriculum reflecting U.S. demographics. Later sections of this chapter will provide additional ideas for educators developing culturally appropriate curricula.

Prerequisites

Several prerequisites must be addressed before a multicultural curriculum can become a reality. First, educators need to determine the extent to which the curriculum presently reflects multicultural content and then make a sincere commitment to the essential principles of a democratic society. These prerequisites cannot be taken lightly. Educators must be committed to a genuine multicultural education curriculum, know the extent to which the goal has already been achieved, and have an appropriate plan to make the curriculum more multicultural in nature. While the curricular aspects can be somewhat objectively measured, determining the degree to which affective areas have been reached proves more difficult. This difficulty, however, should not prevent educators from at least considering and attempting to measure their progress in affective areas. All efforts should focus on translating talk about the multicultural curriculum into actual practice.

Assessing curricula needs

With the idea firmly in mind that the curriculum includes more than just the content taught and the curricular materials used, educators can use several criteria to assess the degree to which the curriculum reflects cultural diversity. Those below provide representative examples of aspects to assess. Perceptive educators will see that these criteria provide an excellent beginning point; however, the criteria should be modified to meet the needs of individual school situations.

Criteria	Yes	No	Areas Needing Attention
1. Multicultural perspectives permeate the entire school curriculum.	___	___	_____
2. Teachers, administrators, and staff members genuinely respect cultural diversity.	___	___	_____
3. Textbooks and curricular materials recognize the value of cultural diversity, gender, and social class differences.	___	___	_____
4. Curricular activities and methods provide learners with opportunities to work cooperatively.	___	___	_____

Criteria	Yes	No	Areas Needing Attention
5. Extracurricular activities provide equal access to all young adolescents, regardless of cultural diversity.	___	___	_____
6. Curricular efforts include bilingual perspectives and provide assistance for students with limited English-speaking skills.	___	___	_____
7. Instructional practices reflect culturally diverse learners' learning styles.	___	___	_____
8. Media center materials reflect diversity of all types.	___	___	_____
9. School policies and expectations accommodate the needs and expectations of culturally diverse learners.	___	___	_____
10. Orientations toward success, motivation, and working for future rewards reflect young adolescents' cultural backgrounds.	___	___	_____
11. Exploratory opportunities and mini-courses reflect cultural diversity.	___	___	_____
12. Teacher advisory programs include opportunities for culturally diverse learners to discuss relevant issues and opportunities for other young adolescents to learn challenges facing culturally diverse youth.	___	___	_____

Other concerns to be addressed include: (1) the involvement of culturally diverse parents and families in the daily school routine; (2) the possible segregation of sports; (3) the cultural diversity of the art and music included in the school; (4) the employment of culturally diverse persons only in minimum wage positions; and (5) the dominance of stereotypical perceptions in the selection of teaching/ learning activities and in teacher expectations.

Determining barriers to multicultural curricular experiences

While some aspects of the curriculum are readily discernible to young adolescents attending a school, other aspects are more subtle, and may be equally influential. Barriers, often well-entrenched, limit culturally diverse students' potential. For example, educators can determine with relative ease whether textbooks and other curricular materials reflect culturally diverse people. Likewise, one can ascertain the effects of tracking and ability grouping. But barriers often exist which are not so easily detected and when justification for them is asked, educators can often (perhaps unwittingly) defend practices which, in reality, pose barriers to culturally diverse learners.

Barriers might be comprised of any number of events, behavior expectations, and attitudes that might appear relatively unobtrusive to majority-culture learners, yet might appear out of character or context for culturally diverse learners. Although trying to list all possible barriers proves difficult, representative examples might include: teacher behaviors and expectations conveyed both verbally and nonverbally; other students' acceptance and attitudes toward culturally diverse learners; and acceptance or lack of acceptance of language differences. In other words, middle and upper class Anglo students might not be surprised when their teacher encourages them to compete and excel in the class, but this exact same teacher expectation might be anathema to Native American learners. Educators must make a deliberate effort to examine their behaviors, both conscious and unconscious, to determine hidden messages or barriers and to assess carefully every aspect of the curriculum and the total school environment to determine whether culturally diverse learners are being given a different message from that sent to Anglo students.

A Proposed Curriculum Model: Academic, Social, and Personal

Allen, Splittgerber, and Manning (1993) carefully examined a number of curriculum models such as the Eichhorn model (Eichhorn, 1966), Alexander and George (1981), George and Alexander (1993), Lounsbury and Vars (1978) and Beane (1993a) and, building upon the strengths of these models, proposed a model focusing on academic, social, and personal dimensions. Their model is especially appropriate for the middle school because the academic dimension addresses young adolescents' cognitive development while the social and personal dimension addresses their psychosocial development. This curriculum model can be expanded to provide a curriculum that reflects cultural diversity.

Defining curricular dimensions and incorporating multicultural perspectives

The **academic dimension** includes the basic content areas of mathematics, language arts, social studies, science, art, music, and the other areas normally taught in the middle school. This dimension seeks to provide young adolescents with knowledge, the ability to think, ethical standards, and opportunities to engage in meaningful work and develop the responsibilities of citizens (Allen, Splittgerber, & Manning, 1993; Carnegie Council on Adolescent Development, 1989). Multiculturalism can become integral in the academic dimension by providing learning experiences which:

1. teach about culturally diverse people, their traditions, customs, and backgrounds;
2. teach that differences should not be equated with being wrong or inferior—differences are enriching to the school and the nation and should be recognized as such;
3. teach the positive contributions of culturally diverse people to our lives today; and
4. teach about the struggles for equality culturally diverse people have had to face in a majority culture society.

The **social dimension** includes the necessary opportunities for socialization, extracurricular activities, and interaction with peers, teachers, and adults in school, home, and community. The goal is to develop a fully socially competent being and involves the teaching of power sharing, negotiation, and joint responsibility. Multiculturalism can be incorporated in the social dimension by:

1. encouraging acceptance of one's own culture;
2. teaching understanding of the challenges of being culturally diverse in a majority culture society;
3. developing an understanding of differences, i.e., differing cultural perspectives toward friendships should not be considered strange or wrong;
4. helping students recognize racism and appreciate how racism and discrimination can have a devastating effect on friendship formation and overall social development; and
5. teaching the importance of interdependence of individuals, groups, cultures, and nations in a global community.

The **personal dimension** includes health, physical education, unified arts, career, and exploratory activities to assist the young adolescent in the development of values and attitudes. Curricular decisions should draw from the experiential background of young adolescents and assist them in dealing with life's challenges. Multiculturalism can be incorporated into the personal dimension by:

1. teaching young adolescents to develop respect for one's cultural background, heritage, customs, and traditions;

2. promoting the necessity of developing a positive cultural identity and provide appropriate experiences;

3. teaching enlightened understandings of diversity and the necessity of examining one's cultural baggage, i.e., myths and stereotypes of others; and

4. helping youngsters to understand and respect their own culture as well as understand and respect others' cultures.

Curricular Areas and Multiculturalism

Individual subject areas

While this section points out ways multiculturalism can be incorporated in various subject areas, it is important to note that the middle school curriculum should adopt an integrated approach. Showing how a multicultural emphasis can be incorporated in individual subject areas is being done for simplicity and to be sure all subject areas are addressed. However, all recent writing on the middle school curriculum (Arnold, 1991; 1993; Beane, 1991; 1992; 1993a; 1993b; George & Alexander, 1993; Lounsbury, 1993; Stevenson, 1992) reinforce the position that middle schools should present an integrated curriculum. Through team planning using thematic units, young adolescents' psychosocial and cognitive development allow them to see relationships among subject areas and how themes cross curricular lines.

Language Arts

- Write Japanese poetic verse such as haiku and tanka
- Read or listen to Dr. Martin Luther King's "I Have a Dream" speech. Discuss ideals, the delivery, and the continuing importance of the speech.
- Read objective and well-written reading materials on customs, traditions, and heritages of culturally diverse people. Resources: Indian Youth of America, 609 Badgerow Building, P.O. Box 2786, Sioux City, IA 51106; The Hispanic Policy Development Project, Suite 310, 1001 Connecticut Ave., NW Washington, DC 20036; and Chicano Family Center (CFC), 7145 Avenue H, Houston, TX 77011
- Work in cooperative learning groups, write a skit or play showing the "positives" of culturally diverse and majority cultures when they work together
- Use choral speaking activities with English as Second Language (ESL) allowing English speaking and language minority students to speak as a group, thus

providing language-minority students with opportunities to develop confidence and learn pronunciations
- Provide listening activities such as "Earth Song," Native American flute music by Carlos Nakai and Native American songs and chants by Brooke Medicine Eagle; and "Song of the Earth Spirit," a Native American poem that can be read aloud (Garfield, 1993)
- Refer to book by Lyn Miller-Lachman (1992), *Our Family, Our Friends, Our World,* (Bowker Publishing, 710pp) which is an annotated guide to significant multicultural books for children and teenagers

Social Studies

- Use the globe to clarify regions and the location of one's cultural backgrounds in the world
- Discuss the term "global village"
- Have students interview parents and grandparents to see where ancestors came from; then, pinpoint those countries on a large map
- Make a timeline showing when large percentages of culturally diverse groups came to the United States — show year or decade and their land of origin
- Study various economic systems to identify advantages and disadvantages of each
- Study effects of racism, discrimination, and stereotypes, generally and in the local community
- Read biographies or reference book accounts of culturally diverse people. e.g.:

> Native American—Jim Thorpe, Vine Deloria, and
> Watyie Strand
> African American—Matthew Henson, Jean Baptiste Pointe
> DuSable, Rosa Parks, and Colin Powell
> Asian American—Laurence Yep, Connie Chung, Thuy Thu
> Lee, and An Wang
> Hispanic American—Henry Cisneros, Caesar Chavez, Juan
> Ramon Jimanez, and Lupe Anguiano

- Discuss various perspectives of a particular culture, e.g. the Hmong and Cambodian people—why they lived where they did in Southeast Asia, the structure of their language, historical perspectives of their cultures, and why they had to leave Laos and Cambodia (Grant & Sleeter, 1989)
- Resources—write Council for Indian Education, 517 Rimrock Road, Billings, MT 59102

Mathematics

- Learn about culturally diverse mathematicians and scientists such as Seki Shinsuke Kowa (1642-1708), David Sanchez (1933-   ), Chien Shiung Wu (1929-   ) and Benjamin Banneker (1731-1806) (Grant & Sleeter, 1989)
- Learn about systems of measurements used in other cultures and compare advantages and disadvantages
- Study units of money from around the world, note similarities and differences
- Convert dollars to other currency systems and let students decide how much money would be needed for lunch at their favorite fast-food restaurant using the various monetary systems
- Learn about cultural influences on measurements and time
- Learn about several calendars such as Christian Calendar, Hebrew Calendar, Islamic Calendar, and Chinese Calendar. Compare and contrast

Science

- Investigate inventors and scientists from non-Anglo cultures and countries
- Examine endangered species from various continents such as Africa and Asia and show differences in how people from those areas and Anglo-Americans view the situation

Art

- Examine art from one's cultural background
- Prepare a mural, collage, or mobile portraying one's cultural background
- Take field trip to art museum with special exhibits focusing on culture
- Interview culturally diverse artists in the community
- Make papier mache' projects illustrating cultural backgrounds
- Create dioramas and murals portraying cultural diversity
- Make covers for books and reports with illustrations depicting cultural diversity
- Make Native American sand paintings and interpret other students' work
- Resources: Write—Chinese Cultural Center, 159 Lexington Ave., New York, NY 10016; or the Southeast Asian Center, 1124-1128 W. Ainslie, Chicago, IL 60640

Music

- Examine music representative of one's cultural background or from other cultural backgrounds
- Study Black Blues artists, i.e., Ma Rainey, Bessie Smith, and Ella Fitzgerald
- Play and reflect upon folk tunes from various cultures and identify common areas and themes

- Read books showing African Americans' contributions to the fine arts—Byran, Ashley. *I'm Going to Sing: Black Spirituals, Vol 2,* Athenum, 1982; and Haskins, James. *Black Theater in America,* Crowell, 1982

Note: For other curricular suggestions, an excellent resource is Grant and Sleeter's *Turning on Learning: Five Approaches for Multicultural Teaching Plans for Race, Class, Gender, and Disability,* Merrill, 1989.

Example of curricular unit reflecting multiculturalism

While the above section identified several ways each subject area could reflect multiculturalism, the following is an example of a multicultural unit on a specific theme.

Multicultural Resource Unit
Unjust Treatment of Culturally Diverse People

African Americans brought to American to be sold into slavery; Native Americans being forced off their lands, Asian Americans, especially Chinese Americans, working on the railroad linking the Missouri River to the Pacific Coast in 1862, Hispanic Americans working in "sweat factories" or working as migrant workers, and Japanese Americans in the aftermath of the bombing of Pearl Harbor.

Objectives/Activities

1. The students will define the following terms: *racism, discrimination,* and *injustice* and identify examples of each that have been inflicted upon several culturally diverse groups.
2. The students will identify three books and/or songs that describe the injustices experienced by culturally diverse groups.
3. The students will develop a timeline showing culturally diverse peoples' responses to unjust treatment i.e., African Americans' March on Washington in 1963.
4. The students will identify three examples of contemporary racism, discrimination, or injustice and list possible solutions for addressing each.

Some of these activities can be carried out by individuals, others in cooperative learning groups or interest-established pairs or triads.

Language Arts

- Read the previously mentioned books and also *The Drinking Gourd* and *Sing Down the Moon* and write a review of each
- Prepare short stories, poems, skits, and plays on the unjust treatment received by many culturally diverse people
- Write and give a speech which a Native American might have given regarding land being taken away
- Keep a class scrapbook of unjust practices currently existing in the United States
- Write a letter to the editor of a newspaper proposing a solution to an injustice being imposed upon people today

Mathematics

- Compile a "numbers" list—acres of land taken away from Native Americans, numbers of African Americans brought to America to work as slaves; numbers of Asian Americans working on the railroad, and numbers of Hispanic Americans working as migrant workers   Compute approximate estimates of money saved by having workers work in low paying jobs in poor working conditions
- Use a bar or pie graph to show numbers of culturally diverse workers in minimum wage paying jobs
- Estimate value of land taken from Native Americans and compare amounts they received (if any amounts were actually paid)

Science

- Study terrain, i.e., land taken away from Native Americans and farming land on which migrant workers grow produce
- Examine climate conditions needed to grow various types of produce and determine the effects on people of these conditions
- Study the climatic conditions (for example, temperature, humidity, heat index) existing in many "sweat shops" and resulting effects on people

Social Studies

- Examine the concepts of racism, injustice, and discrimination and pinpoint both historical and contemporary examples
- Gather information on immigration patterns by decade or some other time frame
- Review America's resistance to immigrants entering the United States [For examples of resistance today, see in *Newsweek's* "Immigration Backlash" (Thomas & Murr, August 9, 1993) in which a poll indicates 60% of Americans think immigration is bad for the nation; and other news magazines reporting on the Haitian and Cuban refugees seeking to come to America in 1994.

- Prepare an essay explaining the melting pot concept and its limitations and how we presently support the salad bowl concept
- Write a position paper for or against the resistance or unjust treatment culturally diverse people received upon arrival to the United States
- Develop a timeline showing each culturally diverse people's important dates or events, i.e., The Emancipation Proclimation.
- Develop a chart listing injustices and offer possible solutions

Art

- Study works of art depicting injustices culturally diverse people have suffered and struggled to overcome
- Create collages, dioramas, and mobiles showing injustices—the bonds of slavery, the plight of Native Americans, and the menial jobs many Asian and Hispanic Americans have been forced to accept
- Study art of various cultures and look for common themes and areas. Resource: *Our Hispanic Heritage.*, Raintree Publishing, 1989, *Diego Rivera: Mexican Muralist.*, Hargrove, J., Children's Press, 1990, or *Inspirations: Stories About Women Artists.*, Sills, Leslie. Albert Whitman Publishing, 1989.
- Examine Native American art and the relationship between art and the chronology (Resource: Highwater, Jamake. *Many Smokes, Many Moons: A Chronology of American Indian History Through Indian Art.* HarperCollins, 1978.)

Music

- Listen to songs of various cultures which have been helps to survival, providing a ray of hope, and/or communicating pain and suffering
- Write lyrics for a familiar melody that deal with a contemporary injustice and offer hope
- Research musical instruments used by slaves and other people suffering from various forms of bondage or ill treatment.
- Develop teaching-learning experiences from using such resources as *Black Music in America: A History Through its People* (Haskins, James, HarperCollins, 1987) or *Shake It to the One That You Love the Best: Play Songs and Lullabies from Black Musical Traditions* (Mattox, Cheryl Warren, Ed., Warren-Mattox Productions, 1990).

Other Resources

Selected books appropriate for 10-15 year olds which can complement this unit on "Unjust Treatment of Culturally Diverse People" include:

African Americans

Adler, David A. *Jackie Robinson: He Was the First.* Holiday House, 1989,

48pp. Nonfiction. This is an accurate and informative account about Jackie Robinson and the time in which he lived.

Anthony Burns: The Defeat and Triumph of a Fugitive Slave. Knopf, 1988, 192pp. Nonfiction. Burns, a runaway slave was jailed in Boston and lost his legal case under the Fugitive Slave Act of 1850.

Hansen, Joyce. *Out From This Place.* Walker, 1988, o.p. Fiction. Easter and Obi escaped enslavement but were captured by Confederate soldiers. Obi escapes and Easter sets out to find him.

Humphrey, Kathryn Long. *Satchel Paige.* Watts, 1988, 128pp. Nonfiction. The story of the most famous of the African Americans who played on the segregated teams of the Negro Baseball League.

Katz, William Loren. *Breaking the Chains: African American Slave Resistance.* Atheneum, 1990, 208pp. Nonfiction. This excellent book confutes the often-held belief that many slaves accepted servitude as a way of life.

Ksoof, Anna. *The Civil Rights Movement and Its Legacy.* Watts, 1989, 112pp. Nonfiction. Kosof recounts her own experiences during the civil rights movement.

Lester, Julius. *This Strange New Feelings.* Dutton/Dial, 1982, 160pp. Fiction. This story tells about Ras and the challenges he faced living in slavery.

Rummell, Jack. *Langston Hughes.* Chelsea House, 1988, 111pp. Nonfiction. Middle level students will appreciate Hughes' determination to leave home and pursue his desire to become a poet.

Asian Americans

Betancourt, Jeanne. *More Than Meets The Eye.* Bantam, 1990, 166pp. Fiction. This book describes the variety of problems Asian Americans face in today's schools.

Bode, Janet. *New Kids on the Block: Oral Histories of Immigrant Teens.* Watts, 1989, 126pp. Non-fiction. Eleven teenagers relate their experiences in regard to leaving their homelands and adjusting to their new life in America.

Brown, Dee Alexander, and Proctor, Linda. *Lonesome Whistle: The Story of the First Transcontinental Railroad.* Holt, Rinehart & Winston, 1980, 144pp. Nonfiction. This book, adapted for young readers, describes the building of the transcontinental railroad and how the Chinese were selected for the work.

Miklowitz, Gloria D. *The War Between the Classes.* Delacorte, 1985, 158pp. Fiction. This book focuses on the injustices resulting from social class structures.

Winter, Frank. H. The Filipinos in America. Lerner, 1988, 71pp. Nonfiction. This readable and balanced book provides an introduction on the fastest-growing Asian immigrant group in the United States.

Native Americans

Ashabranner, Brent. *Morning Star, Black Sun: The Northern Cheyenne Indians and America's Energy Crisis.* Putnam, 1982, 154pp. Nonfiction. Ashabranner examines Native Americans' reverence for the land and how their land was taken away.

Ashabranner, Brent. *To Live in Two Worlds: American Indian Youth Today.* Dodd, Mead, 1984, 149pp. Nonfiction. Ashabranner examines the contemporary lives of a number of Native American teenagers and young adults.

Brown, Dee. *Wounded Knee: An Indian History of the American West.* Dell, 1975, 202pp. Nonfiction. Brown's book corrects the Anglo expansionist view of U.S. history that has been reinforced by the Hollywood stereotypes of the Native American.

Cannon, A. E. *The Shadow Brothers.* Delacorte, 1990, 180pp. Fiction. Cannon shows that Native Americans differ as individuals just like individuals in all cultures.

Gregory, Kristiana. *Jenny of the Tetons.* Harcourt, Brace, Jovanovich, 1989, 119pp. Fiction. Eleven year old Carrie has been orphaned and wounded in a raid and her two younger brothers kidnapped.

Hispanic Americans

Beltra'n Herna'ndez, Irene. *Across the Great River.* Arte Pu'blico, 1989, 136pp. Fiction. Economic hardships force this family to cross the Rio Grande in search of a better life.

Cullison, Alan. *The South Americans.* Chelsea House, 1991, 112pp. Nonfiction. Recent economic and political problems have driven increasing numbers of South Americans north.

Meltzer, Milton. *The Hispanic Americans.* HarperCollins, 1982, 149pp. Nonfiction. Meltzer examines the Hispanic population from both a historical and sociological perspective.

Mills, Claudia. *Luisa's American Dream.* Four Winds, 1981, 155pp. Fiction. Luisa, a fourteen year old girl, hides her Cuban-American background and her nationality.

Pinchot, Jane. *The Mexicans in America.* Lerner, 1989, 94pp. Nonfiction. Pinchot examines issues of importance to Mexican-Americans, i.e., education, immigration, and civil rights.

This partial unit could serve as a beginning point or a skeletal outline. Teachers working in interdisciplinary teams can tap their professional expertise in particular content areas and offer many exciting and productive activities and ideas within this topic.

Other topics for multilevel integrated units

- Contributions of Culturally Diverse People (or a specific cultural group)
- Cultural Traditions: Family and Society (in general or for a specific cultural group)
- Books, Poems and Short Stories for Culturally Diverse Writers (or music or art by musicians and artists, respectively)
- Geography and Locations—Pinpointing Locations of Origin
- Native People of the Southwest (from *A Multicultural Inservice Resource Handbook*, Arizona Department of Education, 1535 West Jefferson Street, Phoenix, AZ 85007)
- African American Scholars: Leaders, Activists, and Writers (from NAACP, 4805 Mount Hope Drive, Baltimore, MD 21215)
- Martin Luther King: A Lifetime of Action (from *Martin Luther King, Jr. Resource Guide,* The State Education Department of New York, Long Island Field Services, #1 Regional Field Services, Room 973 EBA, Albany, NY 12234)
- Contemporary Culturally Diverse Contributors: Civil Rights Activists
- Influential Women and Their Contributions (women in general or women in a specific cultural group)
- Coming to America—Immigration in the 1990s (books especially suggested for fifth and sixth graders include *If You Were There in 1492* (Brenner, Barbara; Macmillan, 1991; *Ajeemah and His Son* (Berry, James; HarperCollins, 1992); and *The Chinese American Family Album* (Hoobler, Dorothy and Thomas; Oxford University Press, 1994) (Fagella, 1994).

Integral aspects of all integrated units

1. Multiculturalism should be reflected in nearly all integrated units and teaching-learning efforts. For example, all topics, both those lending themselves to multiculturalism as well as topics that do not lend themselves to multiculturalism, need to reflect multiculturalism and multicultural issues such as addressing of language and dialect differences, learning styles differences, perspectives of motivation and success, and other cultural differences.

2. Integrated units should include provisions for multiculturalism in other middle school essentials such as teacher advisory sessions, exploratory programs, mini-courses, and teacher-student relationships.

3. Integrated units should include the three aforementioned curricula dimensions. For example, the academic dimension focuses on the specifics of multiculturalism such as content, dates, figures, events, and generally speaking, information of a more concrete nature. The social dimension includes the recognition of interdependence, environment problems, the division of culture and socioeconomic groups, and virtually any aspect related to the society. For example, this dimension focuses on helping young adolescents see the overall effects of injustice on society such as having a group of people financially exploited or emotionally abused. The personal dimension should include individual perspectives such as how individuals perceive the content being taught and how it affects personal lives (for example, how young adolescents might feel subjected to injustices). Again, it is important to point out that these three dimensions are not separate entities. Effective integrated curricula include the academic, social, and personal in a holistic manner where relationships become clear and young adolescents see learning includes more than only facts.

An Integrated Curriculum

There is an emerging curriculum vision, the integrative curriculum, that goes well beyond the original subject-centered and the more recent multi-disciplinary approaches that have characterized the middle school curriculum. This newer vision proposes the idea that genuine learning occurs best when students integrate experiences and insights into their scheme of meaning. Moreover, the most significant learning experiences relate to exploring questions and concerns young people have about themselves and their world. Thus the integrative curriculum begins with questions and concerns and focuses them toward pertinent knowledge and skill (Beane, 1993b). The case for an integrated curriculum in the middle school has been persuasively argued by several writers (Beane, 1991; 1992; 1993a; 1993b; George & Alexander, 1993, Stevenson, 1992; Arnold, 1993). Also, developmentally speaking, young adolescents' need for holistic, integrated understanding invites interdisciplinary treatments of curriculum that have been judged valuable if not essential to their education (Stevenson, 1992).

It is important to note true curriculum integration involves more than simply connecting two or more subject areas while still generally maintaining their identities. Instead the integrative curriculum dissolves and transcends subject area lines, though it does not abandon all the knowledge and skills that have traditionally been defined within the disciplines (Beane, 1993b). This concept of the integrated curriculum allows students to understand relationships and patterns within the curriculum and provides opportunities to synthesize information, solve problems, and apply concepts in multiple subject areas (McEwin & Thomason, 1991).

The integrative curriculum has two basic concepts: First, learning is wasteful and ineffective when it lacks unity and coherence in relation to some larger question or issue. Second, integration is not a concept one can do for another. For full understanding to occur, the integration must be done by young adolescents themselves. Only when learners integrate learning in their own scheme of meanings does authentic learning occur (Beane, 1992).

In support of the integrated curriculum, the NASSP (1993) document, *Achieving Excellence Through the Middle Level Curriculum,* states:

> Curriculum integration helps students "learn how to learn" and helps them become independent, confident students. It should help students develop the broad knowledge base and the skills needed for learning (p. 11).

Beginning points of effective integrated curricula include: recognizing the need for the middle school curriculum to focus on widely shared concerns of young adolescents and of the larger world rather than focusing only on separate subject areas; accepting the position that the primary purpose of the middle school curriculum should be to serve young adolescents; and revising the increasingly popular view that portrays young adolescents as victims of their developmental stage (Beane, 1991).

Curriculum planning in an integrative context begins with collaborative discussion about young adolescents' themes and concerns. Upon identifying a theme and related questions, curriculum planning turns to identifying activities the group may use to answer the questions (Beane, 1992).

At Marquette Middle School (Madison, Wisconsin), teachers conducted a thematic unit that exemplifies the integrated curriculum. The unit began with students listing questions about themselves and their world and then identifying a number of themes based on their questions. Then the students selected one theme, "Living in the Future," and listed possible ways to find answers to the questions. Their planning included naming the knowledge and skills needed to answer the questions (Beane, 1991).

For curriculum integration to become a reality, two crucial aspects warrant recognition. First, integration implies wholeness and unity rather than separation and fragmentation. Second, genuine curricular integration occurs when young people confront personally meaningful questions and engage in related experiences they can integrate into their own system of meaning (Beane, 1991). Several key factors contribute to the effectiveness of integrated themes: relevant topics, clear goals and expectations, flexible activities and grouping strategies, student choice and input, adequate time, field trips, group cooperation, sharing opportunities, and community involvement (Strubbe, 1990).

Integrated curriculum and multiculturalism

Several aspects of the integrated curriculum approach coincide with or complement the multicultural education concept. Consider three of Beane's (1993a) statements:

> The idea of democracy ought to permeate the middle school,
> including its curriculum (p. 65). A second enduring concept
> that ought to permeate the curriculum is that of human dignity
> and the related ideas of freedom, equality, caring, justice, and
> peace (p. 66).
> A third enduring concept, related to the first two, is the
> ostensible prizing of cultural diversity. While the history of
> schooling presents a somewhat bleak picture in this area, we
> are now at a historical moment when this concept may have
> brighter prospects (p. 67).

One can see the similarities of these opinions which are representative of the
new curriculum thrust in middle school curriculum and multicultural education
efforts. To accomplish these goals, educators can provide opportunities for all views,
content, and cultures to be recognized and examined. Young adolescents can learn
about human dignity and the related ideas of freedom, equality, caring, justice, and
peace and can also have opportunities to practice these ideals. Efforts can and
should be undertaken to teach young adolescents to prize cultural diversity.

Content integration involves teachers using examples and information from a
wide variety of cultures and groups to illustrate the key concepts, principles, generalizations, and theories in their subject areas. Some educators view multicultural
education almost solely as content integration which leads some educators to think
multicultural education cannot be integrated into their educational efforts and practices. Likewise, educators can include activities and experiences related to other
dimensions of multicultural education such as reducing prejudice and the promotion of gender equity. Educators genuinely committed to the multicultural education movement can also identify ways to integrate specific content or teach concepts such as justice, democracy, equality, and acceptance (Banks, 1993).

Themes, questions, and concerns

Integrated curricular efforts have often focused on justice, wealth, dignity, the
environment, and prejudice of all kinds. Young adolescents can develop their own
questions and concerns about non-privileged people, explore various cultures with
respect, disdain injustice, debate free speech, demand an end to prejudice, and make

their classrooms a better place than the larger world in which they live (Beane, 1993b).

Themes suggested by students in one class included: "Living in the Future," "Careers, Jobs, and Money," "Conflict," "Environmental Problems," "Sex, Health, and Genetics" (Beane, 1993b). Other organizing themes might include contemporary concerns such as homelessness, hunger, drug abuse, and pollution (McEwin & Thomason, 1991). These suggestions, while not representing multicultural topics per se, can include multiculturalism as young adolescents suggest related questions and concerns such as democracy, freedom, equality, caring, justice, and dignity of all people. Also, educators can be sure learning styles and language differences reflect multiculturalism. In brief, these topics can be examined using more than one cultural perspective and with consideration of the effects of culture and gender on learning and achievement.

Effective multicultural efforts can pose questions and concerns around themes such as:

Immigration—Past and Present

Differences and Similarities: Cultural, Gender, Social Class

Cultural Assimilation

Women and History

Holidays—Customs and Traditions

Leaders, Activists, and Protesters

African American Music: Blues, Jazz, and Rap

Gangs: Appeals and Dangers

Cross-Cultural Friendships

Role Models—Various Cultures

Languages, Dialects, and Nonverbal Communication

Civil Rights Movements

Several criteria should be employed to determine whether a theme is worth the commitment of school time, resources, and energy. Does the theme:

- involve questions from the young adolescents who will carry out the unit?

- involve a concern widely shared by young adolescents, e.g., larger world concerns of clear social significance?

- engage a wide range of knowledge and resources and pose opportunities for in-depth work?

- present possibilities for a wide range of activities and educational experiences?

- present possibilities for action, including action outside the school?(Beane, 1992)

Educators and students selecting themes should consider Arnold's (1991) call for the middle level school curriculum to be rich in meaning. Three characteristics of such a curriculum include:

1. dealing with material which is genuinely important and worth knowing such as the great issues of compassion, justice, freedom, and equality.
2. dealing effectively with values—"What do I personally feel about this issue?" "Are particular positions relative to it right or wrong? Why?"
3. relating both content and methodology to the needs and interests of young adolescents (Arnold, 1991; 1993).

To help in the selection of themes, questions, and concerns Arnold (1991) suggests these questions:

1. What are the really important issues/ideas/concepts/ and principles involved in the topic?
2. What major values/ethical issues are involved?
3. How does this topic relate to students' lives here and now, and how can this relation be extended?
4. How can we develop activities that stimulate inquiry, promote first hand knowledge, and encourage expression, taking into account questions 1-3?

The traditional role of the teacher changes considerably when involved in an integrated curriculum. Among changes are the following:

- playing a more visible role by helping to organize activities, guiding the search for both questions and answers, helping to organize the teaching-learning activities.

- assuming different roles than in the traditional subject-centered curriculum such as becoming more important and vital to learning and achievement.

- helping learners to construct meanings around self and social questions, to use reflective questioning, to identify possible ways to answer them, to reflect upon experiences and interactions, and to generate ways of finding out.

- providing opportunities for students to be engaged in small groups and individual work as well as whole class activities. While whole group work may not be used as much as the other two, students still need opportunities to work together to develop a sense of belonging and collective efficacy.

- providing for active and interactive work with a emphasis placed on discussion, debate, and projects.

- encouraging learners to be concerned with meanings and how they formed those answers rather than right or wrong answers

- employing evaluation methods such as portfolios, journals, project displays, and reflective self-evaluations (Beane, 1992).

Essential Considerations for Curricula Reflecting Multiculturalism

At least five essential considerations determine the extent to which the middle school curriculum reflects multiculturalism and young adolescents' developmental needs. While some might name other considerations, these five considerations seem basic: 10-14 year olds development, the extent to which the curriculum reflects essential middle school concepts, curricular materials, teacher attitudes, and curriculum evaluation.

1. Developmentally appropriate

Young adolescents' psychosocial and cognitive characteristics should provide a developmental basis for all teaching-learning experiences. Young adolescents' cognitive development and their developing ability to think abstractly allow them to understand cultural differences and backgrounds and to see relationships between and among cultures. Perspectives and nuances can be realized that heretofore could not be recognized or understood. For example, young adolescents can increasingly take another person's perspective, i.e., he or she can better understand how racism affects African American learners and can realize personal challenges and societal problems which young adolescents might face. The curriculum should also reflect young adolescents' psychosocial development. More concerned with friendship networks and peer expectations, young adolescents' developing psychosocial abilities allow them to develop friendships across cultural lines. Curricular experiences which reflect psychosocial development provide them with opportunities to socialize, collaborate with others, and participate in peer-tutoring activities.

Providing developmentally appropriate educational experiences is also compatible with the three curricular dimensions: academic, social, and personal. Increasing psychosocial development allows more sophisticated understandings of self and others in the personal and social dimensions, respectively. Likewise, young adolescents' psychosocial and cognitive development allows for increased social interaction, ability to conduct an increased number of academic tasks, higher levels of thought, and a better understanding of self and others.

2. Middle level in nature

The curriculum truly addressing the needs of young adolescents is uniquely "middle school" and includes the concepts embodied in the middle school movement: comprehensive guidance and counseling, exploratory experiences, continuous progress, a distinctive middle school curriculum, and teachers prepared to work with young adolescents and who are expert in the middle school concept. While this might sound too simplistic to even mention, the work of Allen, Splittgerber, and Manning (1993), Beane (1992, 1993a), and George & Alexander (1993) among others, has emphasized the need for a curriculum uniquely geared to the needs of young adolescents. Curriculum that lacks a middle school or multicultural emphasis will not meet the needs of young adolescents, culturally diverse or majority culture. Curriculum developers and teachers need to be constantly vigilant to ensure that the school curriculum reflects both young adolescents' developmental needs and a genuine concern for multiculturalism — a curriculum lacking either one shortchanges the young adolescents it purports to serve.

3. Culturally appropriate teaching-learning materials

Speaking only of textbooks, Banks (1993) writes

> Textbooks have always reflected the myths, hopes and dreams of people with money and power. As African Americans, Hispanics, Asians, and women become more influential, textbooks will increasingly reflect their hopes, dreams, and disappointments. Textbooks will have to survive in the marketplace of a browner America. Because textbooks still carry the curriculum in the nation's public schools, they will remain an important focus for multicultural curriculum reformers (p. 24-25).

Regardless of the curriculum design and teachers' commitment, it is essential that schools use textbooks and other curricular materials which reflect the diversity of our nation. A curriculum genuinely promoting multiculturalism cannot use written materials which teach only about majority culture people, values, and customs. Likewise, curricular materials which present only majority perspectives will not complement other curriculum efforts. Last, appropriate curricula materials, even if multicultural in nature, must also address all three dimensions. Addressing only the academic dimension can teach the content and facts; however, the social and personal dimensions also need to be addressed. Young adolescents need more than factual content such as a list of cultural differences and biographical names and accomplishments.

Textbooks, workbooks, worksheets, and virtually all materials used for teaching have a powerful impact on learners' cognitive and affective domains. Not only is factual information being taught, but these materials also affect students' attitudes and beliefs toward themselves, other people and cultures. Curricular materials with vestiges of stereotyping or outright racism and sexism can have devastating effects on learners and learning outcomes. Young adolescents can easily detect a discrepancy when their educators teach the value of hard work and obtaining a "good" job yet the curricular materials show culturally diverse people only in low paying, menial positions.

Educators selecting curricular materials with objective portrayals of culturally diverse people may contact an organization specializing in bias-free materials such as the *Council on Interracial Books for Children,* 1841 Broadway, Room 500, New York, NY 19923. Another source is *Multicultural Publisher's Exchange,* The Highsmith Company, W5527 Highway 106, P. O. Box 800, Fort Atkinson, WI 53538-0800.

4. Culturally appropriate teacher behaviors

Regardless of curriculum design and instructional materials, the classroom teacher will be the "bottom line" and determining factor in the effort to make multiculturalism an integral part of the curriculum. Adept at distinguishing between teachers' comments and their actual school practices, young adolescents can quickly determine whether a teacher is genuinely sincere. What actual behaviors does the teacher demonstrate? Effective conveyors of multicultural concepts demonstrate knowledge of culturally diverse learners; the skills to communicate effectively with culturally diverse learners and to address their learning styles; and the skills to work with culturally diverse learners' differing value systems.

5. Evaluating curricular efforts

Evaluating the multicultural curriculum to determine overall program strengths and weaknesses, and to assess how well it meets individual learner needs, is almost as important as the actual content and teaching methods being used. One basic criterion is to determine the degree to which teaching and learning situations reflect multiculturalism (Sleeter & Grant, 1988).

Specific items to evaluate include the criteria listed at the beginning of this chapter to assess whether a curriculum reflects the cultural diversity of the nation. Evaluational items which pinpoint strengths and weaknesses include educators respecting diversity, curricular materials, extracurricular activities, instructional practices, and school policies. These few evaluation items provide beginning points for teachers to consider. Teachers who have planned and implemented a curriculum reflecting multiculturalism and who know their own individual school situation have a better idea of items needing evaluation.

Other recommended measures of program effectiveness include oral and written tests (teacher-made and standardized), sociograms, questionnaires, surveys, student projects, interview, anecdotal information, and discussion groups. Indicators such as attendance records, class participation, and incidence of disruptive behavior also provide clues about student acceptance of and interest in the program (California State Department of Education, 1979).

Linguistically Different Learners: Issues and Teaching Strategies

The linguistic diversity of the United States will continue to challenge educators in the 21st century. As one examines the issue of linguistically different learners, the following five generalizations are evident:

1. Significant numbers of culturally diverse groups do not speak a language other than English at home and do not speak English "very well."

2. Linguistic diversity (both limited-English-proficiency and dialects) is a controversial issue dividing much of the nation.

3. Inseparable relationships exist between language and culture.

4. Effective multicultural education programs place considerable emphasis on accepting linguistic diversity and encouraging learners to be bilingual and bidialectical.

5. Teaching linguistically different students requires effective strategies.

Problems with English

Significant percentages of Hispanic, Asian, and Pacific Islander groups indicate problems with the English language. For example, in 1990, about 78 percent of Hispanics spoke a language other than English at home (U.S. Bureau of the Census, 1993d, November); of the 4.1 million Asians five years or older, 56 percent reported having problems with English (U.S. Bureau of the Census, 1993b, September); and of the 78,000 Pacific Islanders five years or older, 25 percent spoke an Asian or Pacific Islander language at home (U.S. Bureau of the Census, 1993c, September). Table 4-1 shows a breakdown of specific cultural groups selected by the U.S. Bureau of the Census.

Table 4-1 : Ability to Speak English: 1990

Cultural Group	Do Not Speak English "Very Well" (%))
Asian and Pacific Islander	55.6
Pacific Islander	33.4
Hawaiian	26.7
Samoan	32.7
Tongan	47.4
Guamanian	24.1
Asian only	56.0
Chinese	60.4
Filipino	35.6
Japanese	57.7
Asian Indian	31.0
Korean	63.5
Vietnamese	65.0
Cambodian	73.2
Hmong	78.1
Laotion	70.2
Thai	58.0
Other Asian	49.9
Hispanic	50.8
Mexican	50.9
Puerto Rican	41.4
Cuban	54.5
Dominican	63.7
Central American	65.5
South American	54.6
Spaniard	31.9

Compiled from: U.S. Bureau of the Census. *We the American... Pacific Islanders,* (1993c, September) C 3.2: AM 3/15, p. 5; *We the American... Asians,* (1993b, September) C 3.2: AM 3/13, p. 5; *We the American... Hispanics,* 1993d, November) C 3.2: AM 3/18 993-2, p.7.

While perceptions of abilities to speak English range from a low of 24.1 (Guamanian) to a high of 78.1 (Hmong), it is clear that many culturally diverse groups do not speak English "very well." It also suggests that significant numbers of culturally diverse learners probably hear a language other than English spoken at home.

A controversial issue

Linguistic diversity is a controversial issue in the United States and a source of divisiveness among its citizens. In some school systems, the number of languages and dialects spoken by learners and their parents is staggering, as the languages of Central and South America, Africa, and Asia combine with the various American dialects. Across the nation, linguistically-different learners are not learning the essential lessons of school, and are not fully participating in the economic, social, and political life of the United States. The problem for linguistically-different learners and their educators will likely grow even more serious over the next decade or two as these learners become the majority in the public schools (Bowman, 1989). The issues are widespread: some suggest linguistically-different learners forsake their native languages while others suggest learning English as a second language. A genuine multicultural education program will teach young adolescents' to hold onto their native languages so they can be bilingual and have access to two cultures (Brynes & Cortez, 1992).

Numerous English dialects, language variations shared by groups of speakers, are spoken throughout the United States. These variations typically correspond to differences among people such as their ethnicity, culture, geographical location, and social class. Dialects may include such variations as Black English, Hawaiian Pidgin English, and rural Appalachian English (Gollnick & Chinn, 1990).

A learner's dialect is closely related to her or his cultural identity and overall self-concept. School programs which are effective with culturally different populations are sufficiently flexible to accommodate a range of dialects that learners bring to school. While speaking a nonstandard dialect may have detrimental economic, social, and educational consequences for students, teachers should still accept, value, and appreciate a student's language (Crawford, 1993).

The issue facing educators centers on appropriate ways to address dialects. Alternatives include (1) accommodate all dialects, based on the assumption they are all equal, (2) insist on learners speaking only one dialect in school, and (3) accept dialects for certain uses but insist upon standard English in other situations. For example, educators should allow dialects in social and recreational situations (e.g., other than formal classroom discourse) yet should encourage students in school settings to use standard English since it is the nation's primary written and spoken language. Such a compromise allows students to use dialects, yet it recognizes the long-term social and economic benefits of being able to function in standard English (Gollnick & Chinn, 1990).

Language and culture: Inseparable relationships

English as a second language and multicultural education are two closely related concepts because a complex relationship exists between language and culture. Young adolescents acquire language through socialization and, in turn, language shapes perception of the physical and social world in which learners live. Consequently, one cannot effectively address linguistic differences without acknowledging and respecting cultural differences. Conversely, one cannot respect cultural differences without acknowledging and respecting the importance of a person's language. Learners think and understand the world in their language, also intricately tied to their identity. Ignoring or devaluing learners' native language denies an important part of the rich past and present cultural experiences learners bring to school. Thus, it is critical for classroom teachers to acknowledge and respect children's home language, whether a completely different language or a variant of English such as a dialect (Brynes & Cortez, 1992).

Multicultural programs emphasizing language diversity

Perceptive educators at the middle level understand how respect for language diversity is a prerequisite to effective multicultural programs. They take several steps to support young adolescents' language by:

1. ensuring linguistically different young adolescents have teachers who are trained to work with second language learners;

2. understanding a student might have sufficient ability in English to socialize in the hallways yet may need support to comprehend academic language usage;

3. relating learning to students' life experiences, prior knowledge, and cultural perspectives;

4. validating, respecting, and building, whenever possible, on students' native language abilities (Perez, 1979); and

5. recognizing that dialects should not be eliminated but rather valued (Crawford, 1993).

Effective strategies for teaching linguistically different learners

While the principles of learners are equally applicable with students whose native language is not English, there are some particular strategies that are effective with such students. O'Malley and Chamot (1990) listed techniques for second language learning:

Sound acquisition—learners can listen carefully to sounds spoken by a teacher, other native speaker, or on a tape. Then, they can practice the sounds by talking aloud and role playing verbal situations;

Grammar—learners can follow or infer rules given in textbooks, compare native languages and English, and practice grammatical structures, both written and oral;

Vocabulary—learners can prepare charts, learn words in context, learn words by association with others, use new words in phrases, and use a dictionary when necessary;

Listening comprehension—learners can listen to the radio, records, television, and movies; and listen for different accents, dialects, and registers;

Learning to talk—learners need to be open to make mistakes, make contact with native speakers, ask for corrections, and learn dialogues;

Learning to write—learners can have pen pals and write frequently using any of the writing forms commonly accepted in schools, and maintain journals; and

Learning to read—learners can read something in English every day, read things that are familiar, read texts at the beginner's level; and look for meaning from context (O'Malley & Chamot, 1990).

Still other strategies useful in teaching linguistically different learners follow.

1. Providing teacher-directed activities during which students listen and respond to effective role models.

2. Providing classrooms in which students follow distinct patterns everyday and have time and environment to concentrate on language and content to be learned.

3. Allowing students to help students, e.g., students may be more likely to ask for language clarification from another student than the teacher or be better able to communicate with another student with similar language skills.

4. Asking for volunteers, then asking for group responses, and last establishing turn-taking that requires all students to participate orally.

5. Taking special care to speak clearly and use concrete references, repetitions, rephrasings, gestures, visual aids, and demonstrations.

6. Providing curricular materials on an appropriate cognitive level—a book written for a kindergarten student should not be given to a sixth grader.

7. Using whole language activities whenever possible so students will have opportunities for rich, meaningful interactions with language, both written and oral (Byrnes & Kiger, 1992).

8. Providing opportunities for *recounts* (essentially extended versions of known information and answer exchanges), *accounts* (narratives generated by the teller to provide new information), *eventcasts* (on-going narratives interesting to both teller and listener), and *stories* (the telling of a narrative) in which learners practice second language skills, both chronologically and thematically (Faltis, 1993).

9. Encouraging students to work in cooperative groups so maximum language interaction can occur, primary language speakers can assist second language learners and provide role models;.

10. Assigning appropriate books to be read aloud so linguistically different learners can hear pronunciations and words in context.

11. Allowing students to read books and then give oral book reports to small groups—second language learners can have role models and can practice English skills.

12. Allowing learners to write—messages, letters, cards, and notes—to be read in English.

13. Including listening centers with records and tapes so second language learners can practice listening skills and learn English simultaneously.

14. Allowing a panel of reporters or reviewers to interview a person or imaginary author in English and clarifying unclear language points.

15. Allowing students to prepare radio or television broadcasts that include book talks, advertisements for books and other products, or reading selections from books (Crawford, 1993).

While this section only provides representative examples of strategies for teaching linguistically different learners, educators will find more help in these books: Leslie W. Crawford's *Language and Literacy Learning in Multicultural Classrooms* (Allyn and Bacon, 1993), Christian J. Faltis' *Joinfostering: Adapting Teaching Strategies for the Multilingual Classroom* (Merrill, 1993), and J. Michael O'Malley's and Anna Uhl Chamot's *Learning Strategies in Second Language Acquisition* (Cambridge University Press, 1990).

Summary

Two powerful emphases are currently influencing the middle school movement, both holding tremendous potential for helping young adolescents to become more knowledgeable and more respectful of others' differences. First, middle level educators are now seriously examining the curriculum itself in an attempt to determine curricular experiences young adolescents need and also to determine the most effective curricular designs to provide the experiences. Second, educators are increasingly seeing the need for having multiculturalism permeate the curriculum rather than being restricted to a multicultural week or an isolated unit of study.

It is indeed fortuitous that these two emphases are occurring simultaneously—they complement each other, multiculturalism adds an affective domain to content being studied, and both are contributing to young adolescents becoming better informed and more caring citizens. While considerable progress has been made toward these two emphases, they have not been reached to a degree middle school educators can feel young adolescents' needs have been met. The challenge continues, and as more light is shed on the middle school curriculum and more effective methods of permeating the curriculum with multiculturalism are discovered, teaching and learning experiences can better meet all the needs of young adolescents. ◆

5

Resources on Multicultural Education

On the day when we can truly trust one another, there will be peace on earth.

Resources on Multicultural Education 5

A number of professional association and organizations, resource centers, and state departments of education have evidenced increased interest in multicultural education and the importance of learners' forming accurate perceptions of others cultural, ethnic, and social class differences.

This chapter provides readers with (1) names and addresses of these professional organizations, youth and cultural organizations, resource centers, and several departments of education working to improve the lives of culturally diverse learners, especially young adolescents; and (2) an annotated bibliography of selected articles and books for readers desiring additional information.

Selected Professional Organizations

National Middle School Association, 2600 Corporate Exchange Drive, Suite 370, Columbus, OH 43231. The leading organization working for the education and overall welfare of young adolescents, the National Middle School Association publishes the *Middle School Journal* five times a year and *High Strides, The Bimonthly Report on Urban Middle Grades,* plus other newsletters. The association also sponsors professional developmental sessions throughout the United States and sponsors an annual national convention. More than forty monographs and books are available on virtually all topics addressed in this monograph. The Association has a standing committee on Diverse Cultural, Racial, and Ethnic Concerns, and one on Urban Education.

Association for Childhood Education International, 11501 Georgia Avenue, Suite 315, Wheaton, MD 20902. ACEI works for the welfare of children from infancy through early adolescence and publishes *Childhood Education.* ACEI has a sectional organization for members especially interested in young adolescents. Called the Division for Later Childhood/Early Adolescence, this division publishes a quarterly publication called *Focus on Later Childhood/Early Adolescence.* ACEI sponsors an Annual Study Conference and publishes a wealth of materials for children and young adolescents.

National Association of Secondary School Principals, 1904 Association Drive, Reston, VA 22091. NASSP publishes the *NASSP Bulletin* and other publications related to middle level education such as *Achieving Excellence Through the Middle Level Curriculum* (NASSP, 1993), "Cultural and Linguistic Democracy: A Challenge for Today's Schools" (NASSP, 1992) and *Middle Level Education's Responsibilities for Intellectual Development* (NASSP, 1989). Other multicultural materials include "The World Calendar," "The Cultural and Festival Days of the World Poster," and "The Ethnic Cultures of America Calendar." While primarily focusing on addressing the needs of administrators, NASSP is committed to middle level education.

Association for Supervision and Curriculum Development, 1250 N. Pitt Street, Alexandria, VA 22314-1403. ASCD publishes *Educational Leadership* monthly September through May except bimonthly December/January. The organization sponsors professional development sessions across the United States and sponsors an annual conference. ASCD publishes a wealth of publications on a number of topics related to middle school education and multicultural education.

National Association of Elementary School Principals, 1015 Duke Street, Alexandria, VA 22314. NAESP publishes *Principal* five times annually and a number of other papers and monographs. Each issue of *Principal* includes "Middle School Notes" and examines issues critical in the United States such as multicultural education.

National Council for the Social Studies, 3501 Newark Street NW, Washington, DC 20016. NCSS publishes a number of articles on multicultural education. For example, the organization's journal, *Social Education,* (April/May 1992 issue) published an article on "Multicultural/Global Education: An Educational Agenda for the Rights of the Child."

National Council of Teachers of English, 1111 Kenyon Road, Urbana, IL 61801. NCTE publishes *Language Arts* and the *English Journal* which focus on elementary and secondary education, respectively. However, both journals include articles on middle level schooling. Also, both journals include topics focusing directly on multicultural issues.

Organizations Working for the Welfare of Culturally Diverse Groups

The following organizations are only representative examples of organizations working for the welfare of culturally diverse groups. There are dozens and dozens of other organizations offering services and materials—far too many to list in this section. Readers wanting names and addresses of other organizations should consult: Daniels, P.N., & Schwartz, C.A. (Eds.). (1994). *Encyclopedia of Associations.* (28th ed.). Washington, DC: Gale Research. Volume 1 National Organizations of the United States (Part 1 - Entries 1-10,317; Part 2 - Entries 10,318-22,709; Part 3 - Name and Keyword Index) and Volume 2 - Geographical and Executive Indexes.

Native American

Native American Rights Fund, 1506 Broadway, Boulder, CO 80302-6296. As the organization's name implies, the Native American Rights Fund (NARF) focuses on legal concerns facing Native Americans and has represented Indian tribes in nearly very state in the nation. The organization offers a *Native American Legal Review* and an *Annual Report* describing various activities.

Indian Youth of America, 609 Badgerow Building, P. O. Box 2786, Sioux City, IA 51106. This organization seeks to improve the lives of Native American children through projects, programs, and a resource center.

Council for Indian Education, 517 Rimrock Road, Billings, MT 59102. The Council for Indian Education promotes higher standards of education for Native Americans, quality children's literature in the culture, and publishes books on Native American life, both past and present.

National Indian Education Association, 1819 H. Street NW, Suite 800, Washington, DC 20006. The primary purpose of this organization is the exchange of ideas, techniques, and research methods among participants in Native American education.

Coalition for Indian Education (CIE), 3620 Wyoming Blvd., NE, Ste 206, Albuquerque, NM 87111. The Coalition works to ensure that education, health, and other programs are effective and of high quality. The organization offers services, training, and technical assistance and publishes the CIE newsletter and *Current Issues in Indian Education.*

North American Indian Association (NAIA), 22270 Plymouth Road, Detroit, MI 48239. NAIA's objectives include establishing a meeting center for Native Americans; preserving and promoting Native American culture; assisting Native Americans in obtaining higher education; helping others in time of need; and working for the betterment of all Native Americans. The organization provides employment and training programs, counseling services, scholarship, welfare, and education funds.

United Native Americans (UNA), 2434 Faria Avenue, Pinole, CA 94564. United Native Americans seeks to promote the general welfare of Native Americans, establish education scholarships, counseling services, and sells historic posters of Native Americans. The organization publishes *Warpath* monthly and sponsors an annual meeting.

African American

National Association for the Advancement of Colored People, 4805 Mount Hope Drive, Baltimore, MD 21215-3297. NAACP offers many fine materials such as readings for both students and teachers, suggestions for Black History month, Black History Read-a-Thons, and lists of African American book publishers and museums.

National Black Child Development Institute, 1463 Rhode Island Ave., NW, Washington, DC 20005. This organization is dedicated to improving the quality of life for African American children and youth and focuses on issues such as health, child welfare, education, and child care.

Minority Caucus of Family Services American, 34-1/2 Beacon Street, Boston, MA 02108. This organization participates in policy-making groups, works toward the needs of minority families, and helps combat racism.

National Black Youth Leadership Council, 250 W. 54th Street, Suite 800, New York, NY 10019. This council provides training and motivation workshops, resources, information, skills, and strategies for fostering leadership.

Afro-Americans Cultural Foundation (AACF), 10 Fiske Place, Ste. 204-206, Mt. Vernon, NY 10550. AACF works to improve self-esteem of Afro-Americans; to improve Anglo Americans' attitudes toward Afro-Americans; and to sponsor an annual workshop called Institute of Racism. Also, AACF works to raise levels of awareness of the potentials and problems facing Afro-Americans and offers a number of publications.

Center for Urban Black Studies, (CUBC), Graduate Theological Union, 2465 LeConte Avenue, Berkeley, CA 94709. This organization provides resources to help with urban community life and oppressed minority people; and develops and offers courses, seminars, and training programs dealing with issues of race, social justice, and urban life.

Black Resources Information Coordinating Services, 614 Howard Ave., Tallahassee, FL 32304. This service focuses on information by and about African Americans, aids in genealogical research, acts as a referral and consulting agency, offers bibliographical services and lecture demonstrations on the African American culture, sponsors seminars and workshops, conducts a national exchange library of 8,000 items, and publishes several newsletters.

Asian American

Chinese Cultural Center, 159 Lexington Ave., New York, NY 10016. The Cultural Center provides classes, and library and information services to promote better understanding of the Chinese culture.

Chinese Cultural Association, P. O. Box 1272, Palo Alto, CA 94302. This worldwide organization promotes communication and better understanding between the Chinese and people of other cultures.

Southeast Asian Center, 1124-1128 W. Ainslie, Chicago, IL 60640. The Southeast Asian Center promotes the independence and well-being of Lao, Hmong, Cambodian, Vietnamese, and Chinese peoples.

Asian American Arts Alliance (AAAA), 339 Lafayette St. 3rd. Floor, New York, NY 10012. Consisting of artists, organizations, corporations, and interested others, AAAA promotes advocacy, support and recognition of Asian American arts and provides information and support services for other organizations. AAAA has several publications, conducts education seminars and workshops, and maintains a library.

Asian American Arts Centre, 26 Bowery St. New York, NY 10013. The Centre supports exhibitions of traditional and contemporary Asian American arts including dance, music, performance, and poetry; conducts educational programs; and maintains an archive of Asian American visual arts.

Filipinas Americas Science and Art Foundation (FASAF), 1209 Park Avenue, New York, NY 10128. Serving as a resource center, FASAF sponsors activities designed to increase appreciation of North and South Americans, Philippine, and Asian cultures; sponsors little-known artists in art, music and science; organizes art shows, seminars and competitions; and conducts specialized educational events, children's services and charitable programs; as well as operates a library of music, art, and science.

Hispanic American

Association of Hispanic Arts (AHA), 200 E. 87th Street, New York, NY 10028. Founded in 1975, AHA promotes the general concept of Hispanic arts, specifically dance, music, art, and theatrical performances.

Hispanic Institute for the Performing Arts (HIFPA), P. O. Box 32249, Calvert Station, Washington, DC 20007. HIFPA began in 1981, and seeks to promote a better understanding of Hispanics by conducting educational and cultural activities.

Puerto Rican Family Institute (PRFI), 116 W. 19th Street, New York, NY 10011. This organization was established in 1960 for the preservation of the health, well-being, and integrity of Puerto Ricans and other Hispanic families in the United States.

Chicano Family Center (CFC), 7145 Avenue H, Houston, TX 77011. CFC, founded in 1971, seeks to enhance understanding and appreciation of the Chicano culture.

Hispanic Society of America, 613 West 155th Street, New York, NY 10032. The Hispanic Society of America strives to promote the Hispanic culture by publishing and disseminating a number of general interest books, bibliographies, biographies, and visual aids. The Hispanic Society will be a valuable resource when educators plan and implement multicultural education experiences or units addressing only the Hispanic culture.

State Departments Emplasizing Cultural Diversity

Arizona Department of Education, 1535 West Jefferson Street, Phoenix, AZ 85007. The Arizona Department of Education has produced a book, *A Multicultural Inservice Resource Handbook: A List for Administrators and Teachers in Arizona,* which lists and describes many multicultural resources for teachers. Examples include *Cultural Awareness Teaching Techniques, Strategies for Teaching Limited English Proficient Students,* and *Native People of the Southwest: A Curriculum.*

California Department of Education, 721 Capitol Mall, P.O. Box 271, Sacramento, CA 95802-0271. Because California has many multicultural populations, the state has committed to helping culturally diverse learners and their educators. It is recommended that readers order the Departments complete publication catalog, *Publications Catalog - Educational Resources;* however, selected titles related to multicultural education include *Images: A Workbook for Enhancing Self-esteem and Promoting Career Preparation, Especially Black Girls, Martin Luther King, Jr.,* and a number of publications on teaching limited-English-proficiency learners.

Florida State Department of Education, 325 Gaines Street, Tallahassee, FL 32399. The Florida State Department of Education publishes a number of publications focusing on multicultural education and improving the educational experiences of culturally diverse learners as well as learners from the majority culture. One such publication is "Technical Assistance Paper No. 9" which focuses on multicultural teaching strategies.

New York Department of Education, 111 Education Building, Washington Ave., Albany, NY 12234. The New York State Department of Education published the *Regents' Policy Statement on Middle-Level Education and School with Middle-Level Grades* and *Resource Monograph on the Middle Grades* which focuses on pupils, programs, and processes. The Department also provides publications on multicultural education. Examples include *Black History Month: A Reflection and Recognition of the African American Family, Martin Luther King: Resource Guide, Promoting Self-Esteem in Young Women,* and *Our Nation, Many Peoples: A Declaration of Cultural Independence.*

Ohio Department of Education, Division of Elementary and Secondary Education, 65 South Front Street, Columbus, OH 43215. The Ohio Department of Education has published a book, *Citizenship, Multicultural, and Human Relations Education* which provides a wealth of instructional activities to teach students to better understand others and to develop positive interpersonal relations.

Texas Education Agency, Publications Distribution, 1701 Congress Avenue, Austin, TX 78701-1494. The Texas Education Agency offers a booklet, *Major Publications of the Texas Education Agency,* which lists several publications on bilingual education, written in both English and Spanish.

Selected National Resource Centers

National Resource Center for Middle Grades/High School Education, University of South Florida, College of Education, 4202 Fowler Avenue, Tampa, FL 33620. This Center provides a variety of products products and services including advisory programs, teaching materials, workshop offerings, and reproducible interdisciplinary units, some of which have a multicultural emphasis.

Center for Early Adolescence, University of North Carolina at Chapel Hill, Suite 223, Carr Mill Mall, Carrboro, NC 27150. The Center for Early Adolescence provides publications, various services, and workshops. The Center is concerned with all areas of early adolescence development and those issues related to young adolescents living healthy and productive lives.

Center for Education of the Young Adolescent, University of Wisconsin— Platteville, 1 University Plaza, Platteville, WI 53818-3099. This Center publishes the *Middle Link* quarterly and a number of brochures and holds a popular summer institute.

Other Selected Organizations

Carnegie Council on Adolescent Development, 437 Madison Avenue, New York, NY 10022. The Carnegie Council on Adolescent Development published *Turning Points: Preparing American Youth for the 21st Century,* which provided a detailed examination of the schools young adolescents need. The publication is "must" reading for middle level educators. Many aspects have implications for multicultural education such as communities of learning, ensuring success for all students, reengaging parents and families, preparing a good citizen and teaching young adolescents to be caring and ethical.

Society for the Study of Multi-Ethnic Literature of the U.S., 132A McIver Building, Department of English, University of North Carolina—Greensboro, Greensboro, NC 27412. MELUS includes educators and students seeking to enrich curricula by countering the notion that American literature is solely a product of

English, Scottish, and Irish immigrants. The organization publishes a quarterly journal and *News Notes* three times per year and sponsors an annual meeting.

Association of Multi-Ethnic Americans, P. O. Box 191726, San Francisco, CA 94119-1726. This association publishes *Melange* quarterly, sponsors an annual meeting, and represents interracial/multi-ethnic families and individuals. It also conducts education programs and promotes the advancement of multi-ethnic children and adults.

National Urban League, 500 E. 62nd. New York, NY 10021. The National Urban League has national programs that address a number of problems and challenges facing urban youth of all cultures.

Children's Defense Fund, 25 E. Street NW, Washington, DC 20001. The Children's Defense Fund published *Making the Middle Grades Work* which focused on the problems of middle grades students, the need for better middle level schooling and specific state initiatives to improve middle level education. The organization focuses on several problems related in young adolescents such as poverty, drug abuse, and teenage pregnancy.

Annotated Bibliography: Selected Research and Publications

Abt-Perkins, D., & Gomez, M.C. (1993). A good place to begin: Examining our personal perspectives. *Language Arts, 70,* 193-202. These authors believe that teaching multiculturally begins with looking and understanding our own perspectives of culture and education.

Balch, O. (1991). What is the middle school's new role in teaching cultural literacy? *Middle School Journal, 22*(5), 38-40. Balch maintains that literacy requires textbooks, especially in science, English, social science, and fine arts be multiethnic.

Banks, J., & Banks, C. A. M. (1993). *Multicultural education: Issues and perspectives* (2nd ed.). Boston: Allyn and Bacon. Banks, a leader in the multicultural education movement, examines history, goals, and practices; conceptual issues, and a host of other topics relating to teaching learners about our increasingly culturally diverse society.

Baruth, L. G., & Manning, M. L. (1992). *Multicultural education of children and adolescents.* Boston: Allyn and Bacon. These authors examine the four most populous cultural groups in the U.S., look at curriculum and instruction, and include an entire chapter on involving parents and families.

Butler, D. A., & Sperry, S. (1991). Gender issues and the middle level curriculum. *Middle School Journal, 23*(2), 18-23. Butler and Sperry focused on issues such as gender equity, female development, and pedagogical suggestions for gender equity.

Byrnes, D. A., & Kiger, G. (Eds.) (1992). *Common bonds: Anti-bias teaching on a diverse society.* Wheaton, MD: Association for Childhood Education International. Brynes and Kiger examine the growing diversity in our schools, identify various forms of cultural diversity, and suggest ways teachers can build inclusive classroom environments.

Cheney, L. V. (1993). Multicultural education done right. *Change, 25*(1), 8-10. While Cheney's article focuses on higher education, her principles apply to all levels of education.

Crawford, L. W. (1993). *Language and literacy learning in multicultural classrooms.* Boston: Allyn and Bacon. Crawford looks at foundations for language and literacy; preparing to teach in multicultural classrooms; multicultural instructional programs; and assessing and evaluating language and literacy in multicultural classrooms.

Deegan, J. G. (1992). Understanding vulnerable friendships in fifth grade culturally diverse classrooms. *Middle School Journal, 23*(4), 21-25. Deegan looks at three students with vulnerable friendships and offers suggestions for facilitating the changing dynamics of friendships.

Diaz, C. F. (Ed.) (1992). *Multicultural education for the 21st century.* Washington: National Education Association. Diaz includes thirteen chapters in this edited volume which focuses on multicultural education as a concept, effective teaching practices, institutional climate, learning styles, language diversity, and reducing prejudice.

Faltis, C. J. (1993). *Joinfostering: Adapting teaching strategies for the multilingual classroom.* Columbus, OH: Merrill. Faltis examines language diversity in schools and offers suggestions for classroom environments, integrating language and content instruction, small groupwork, and building bridges between parents and schools.

Garfield, S. (1993). Fostering cross-cultural understanding. *Teaching K-8, 23*(7), 45-47. Garfield provides an excellent integrated thematic unit based on the novel *Light in the Forest* by Conrad Richter.

Hepburn, M. A. (1993). Concepts of pluralism and the implications for citizenship education. *Social Studies, 84*(1), 20-26. Hepburn examines the roots of pluralism, the melting pot idea, and the prospects for the future.

Hernandez, H. (1989). *Multicultural education: A teacher's guide to content and process.* Columbus, OH: Merrill. Hernandez examines culture, classroom processes, bilingualism, special and gifted education, instructional materials, and home, neighborhood, and community.

Mackey, B. J. (1990). Cross-age tutoring: Students teaching students. *Middle School Journal, 22*(1), 24-26. Mackey looks at the preparation and planning of cross-age tutors, and the benefits for all learners. As described in the article, students tutoring other students can be an ideal means of getting students from different cultures to work together.

Manning, M. L. (1989). Multicultural education. *Middle School Journal, 21*(1), 14-16. Using a question and answer format, Manning examines several aspects of multicultural education such as definitions, its importance, goals, fundamentals, and unresolved issues.

Manning, M. L., & Lucking, R. (1993). Cooperative learning and multicultural classrooms. *The Clearing House, 67,* 12-16. Manning and Lucking examine cooperative learning only from a cultural perspective and show how students working cooperatively have special benefits for culturally diverse learners.

Manning, M. L., & Baruth, L. G. (1991). Appreciating cultural diversity in the classroom. *Kappa Delta Pi Record, 27*(4), 104-107. Manning and Baruth examine Native, African, Asian, and Hispanic American family traditions, customs, and expectations.

May, S. A. (1993). Redeeming multicultural education. *Language Arts, 70,* 364-372. May reports on a school's efforts to provide learners with significant multicultural education experiences and which recognizes and affirms cultural respect.

Middle School Journal, 21(1). The September 1989 issue of the Middle School Journal focused approximately twenty-two articles on multicultural education.

Rothenberg, D. (1993). Multicultural education (ERIC/EECE Report). *Middle School Journal, 24*(4), 73-75. Rothenberg reviews a number of ERIC/EECE documents on multicultural education, culturally appropriate pedagogy, lessons from Africa, and multicultural mathematics education.

Stavro, S. (1993). Developing intercultural sensitivity in the middle years. *Middle School Journal, 24*(4), 70-72. Stavro discusses the critical age theory of developing appropriate cultural attitudes and offers a transactional model for increasing awareness and sensitivity in the classroom

Teidt, P. L., & Teidt, I. M. (1990). *Multicultural teaching: A handbook of activities, information, and resources* (3rd ed.). Boston: Allyn and Bacon. Tiedt and Tiedt provide over four hundred pages of activities and resources designed for multicultural teaching.

Valentin, T. (1993). English as a second language: get ready for the onslaught. *NASSP Bulletin, 76*(5), 30-38. Valentin urges educators teaching in multicultural areas to work with the community and churches and prepare staff members, students and parents.

Yokota, J. (1993). Issues in selecting multicultural children's literature. *Language Arts, 70,* 156-167. Yokota examines trends in children's literature and such issues as making sure the curriculum includes books other than the mainstream cultures. The authors also include an excellent bibliography of children's multicultural books.

Summary

Middle school educators face two challenges in dealing with multicultural education, both of which can be met with some degree of success. First, multicultural education is a relatively recent concept on the educational front and is, therefore, not widely understood or appreciated by many practicing teachers. Second, the early adolescence years are particularly crucial for developing acceptance of others as well as making a commitment to reduce racism, discrimination, and prejudice. Educators are also challenged to provide multicultural education experiences which assist young adolescents in accepting and appreciating differences among people. A number of resources are available to help middle school educators plan and implement multicultural education programs. University resource centers, professional associations, organizations promoting the welfare of specific cultural groups, and an increasing number of books and journal articles can provide useful information, materials, and instructional strategies. Also, for multicultural education to permeate all areas of the school, educators need to take collaborative action to gather resources and information and, then, work as a group to plan and implement multicultural education programs. The resources suggested in this chapter should be considered a beginning point rather than an exhaustive list. Educators will need to add to the list as they locate new sources of information and materials. ◆

REFERENCES

Abt-Perkins, D., & Gomez, M. C. (1993). A good place to begin—Examining our personal perspectives. *Language Arts, 70,* 193-202.

Alexander, C. (1989). Gender differences in adolescent health concerns and self-assessed health. *Journal of Early Adolescence, 9,* 467-479.

Alexander, W. M., & George, P. S. (1981). *The exemplary middle school.* New York: Holt, Rinehart and Winston.

Allen, H. A., Splittgerber, F. L., & Manning, M. L. (1993) *Teaching and learning in the middle level school.* Columbus, OH: Merrill.

Allport, G. W. (1979). *The nature of prejudice.* (25th anniversary edition). Reading, MA: Addison-Wesley.

Allport, G. W. (1954). *The nature of prejudice.* Reading, MA: Addison-Wesley.

America's first..., (1989). *Census and you, 24* (3), 1.

Appleton, N. (1983). *Cultural pluralism in America.* White Plains, NY: Longman.

Arnold, J. (1993). A curriculum to empower young adolescents. *Midpoints.* Columbus, OH: National Middle School Association.

Arnold, J. (1991). Towards a middle level curriculum rich in meaning. *Middle School Journal, 23* (2), 8-12.

Arnold, J. (1990). *Visions of teaching and learning: 80 exemplary middle level projects.* Columbus, OH: National Middle School Association.

Atkinson, D. R., Morten, G., & Sue, D. W. (1989). *Counseling American minorities: A cross-cultural perspective* (3rd ed.). Dubuque, IA: Wm. C. Brown.

Attneave, C. (1982). American Indians and Alaska native families: Emigrants in the homeland. In M. McGoldrick, J.H. Pearce, & J. Giordano (Eds.), *Ethnicity and family therapy* (pp. 55-83). New York: Guilford.

Axelson, J. A. (1985). *Counseling and development in a multicultural society.* Monterey, CA: Brooks/Cole.

Balch, O. (1991). What is the middle school's new role in teaching cultural literacy? *Middle School Journal, 22* (5), 38-40.

Banks, J. A. (1981). *Education in the 80's: Multiethnic education.* Washington, DC: National Education Association.

Banks, J. A. (1991). *Teaching strategies for ethnic studies* (5th ed.). Boston: Allyn and Bacon.

Banks, J. A. (1992). Multicultural education: Nature, challenges, and opportunities. In C. F. Diaz (Ed.), *Multicultural education for the 21st century* (pp. 23-37). Washington: National Education Association.

Banks, J. A. (1993). Multicultural education: Progress and prospects. *Phi Delta Kappan, 75,* 22-28.

Banks, J. A., & Banks, C. A. M. (1993). *Multicultural education: Issues and perspectives* (2nd ed.). Boston: Allyn and Bacon.

Baruth, L. G., & Manning, M. L. (1992). *Multicultural education of children and adolescents.* Boston: Allyn and Bacon.

Beane, J. A., & Lipka, R. P. (1987). *When the kids come first: Enhancing self-esteem.* Columbus, OH: National Middle School Association.

Beane, J. A. (1991). Middle school: The natural home of integrated curriculum. *Educational Leadership, 49* (2), 9-13.

Beane, J. A. (1992). Turning the floor over: Reflections on a middle school curriculum. *Middle School Journal, 23* (3), 34-40.

Beane, J. A. (1993a). *A middle school curriculum: From rhetoric to reality* (2nd ed.). Columbus, OH: National Middle School Association.

Beane, J. A. (1993b). Problems and possibilities for an integrative curriculum. *Middle School Journal, 25* (1), 18-23.

Benenson, J. F. (1990). Gender differences in social networks. *Journal of Early Adolescence, 10,* 472-495.

Black population is growing... (1988, June). *Census and You, 23* (6), 3-4.

Bodinger-deUriarte, C. (1991, December). Hate crime: The rise of hate crime on school campus. *Research Bulletin (no. 10),* 1-6.

Bowman, B. T. (1989). Educating language-minority children: Challenges and opportunities. *Phi Delta Kappan, 71,* 118-120.

Boykin, A. W. (1982). Task variability and the performance of black and white school children. *Journal of Black Studies, 12,* 469-485.

Breakfast club creates understanding and respect among students. (1994, April). *The Multicultural Link,* p. 1.

Brynes, D. A., & Cortez, D. (1992). Language diversity in the classroom. In D.A. Brynes & G. Kiger (Eds.), *Common bonds: Anti-bias teaching in a diverse society* (pp. 71-85). Wheaton, MD: Association for Childhood Education International.

Byrnes, D. A., & Kiger, G. (Eds.) (1992). *Common bonds: Anti-bias teaching in a diverse society.* Wheaton, MD: Association for Childhood Education International.

Butler, D. A., & Sperry, S. (1991). Gender issues and the middle school curriculum. *Middle School Journal, 23* (2), 18-23.

California State Department of Education. (1987). *Caught in the middle.* Sacramento, CA: Author.

Carew, J. V., & Lightfoot, D. L. (1979). *Beyond bias: Perspectives on classrooms.* Cambridge: Harvard.

Carnegie Council on Adolescent Development. (1989). *Turning points: Preparing American youth for the 21st century.* New York: Author.

Chavkin, N. F. (1989). Debunking the myth about minority parents. *Educational Horizons, 67* (4), 119-123.

Cheney, L. V. (1993). Multicultural education done right. *Change, 25* (1), 8-10.

Christensen, E. W. (1989). Counseling Puerto Ricans: Some cultural considerations. In D. R. Atkinson, G. Morten, & D. W. Sue (Eds.) *Counseling American minorities: A cross-cultural perspective* (3rd ed.) (pp. 205-212). Dubuque, IA: W. C. Brown.

Compton, M. F., & Hawn, H. C. (1993). *Exploration: The total curriculum.* Columbus, OH: National Middle School Association.

Connors, N. A. (1992). Teacher advisory: The fourth R. In J. L. Irwin (Ed.) *Transforming middle level education* (pp. 162-178). Boston: Allyn and Bacon.

Cordova I. R., & Love, R. (1987). Multicultural education: Issues, concerns, and commitments. *The North Central Association Quarterly, 61,* 391-398.

Crawford, L. W. (1993). *Language and literacy learning in multicultural classrooms.* Boston: Allyn and Bacon.

Davenport, D. S., & Yurich, J. M. (1991). Multicultural gender issues. *Journal of Counseling and Development, 70,* 64-71.

Davis, B. C. (1989). A successful parent involvement program. *Educational Leadership, 47* (2), 21-23.

Davis, F. J. (1978). *Minority-dominant relations: A sociological analysis.* Arlington Heights, IL: AHM Publishing.

Dawson, M. M. (1987). Beyond ability grouping: A review of the effectiveness of ability grouping and its alternatives. *School Psychology Review, 16,* 348-369.

Deegan, J. G. (1992). Understanding vulnerable friendships in fifth grade culturally diverse classrooms. *Middle School Journal, 23* (4), 21-25.

Dentzler, E., & Wheelock, A. (1990). *Locked in/locked out: Tracking and placement practices in Boston public schools.* Boston: Massachusetts Advocacy Center.

Department of the Secretary of State, Ottawa (1987). *Multiculturalism: Being Canadian.* Author.

Diaz, C. (1992). *Multicultural education for the 21st century.* Washington: National Education Association.

Dorman, G. (1984). *The middle grades assessment program.* Carrboro, NC: Center for Early Adolescence.

DuBois, D. L., & Hirsch, B. J. (1990). School and neighborhood friendship patterns of blacks and whites in early adolescence. *Child Development, 61,* 524-536.

Duquette, G. (1987). Culture and the French Canadian: A question of survival. In *Theory, research, and applications: Selected papers from the annual meeting of the National Association for Bilingual Education,* Denver, CO, March 30-April 13, 1987, ED 336 974.

Eichhorn, D. (1966). *The middle school.* New York: Center for Applied Research in Education.

Faggella, K. (1994). Coming to America. *Instructor, 103*(6), 42-43.

Faltis, C. J. (1993). *Joinfostering: Adapting teaching strategies for the multilingual classroom.* Columbus, OH: Merrill.

Fehr, D. E. (1993). When faculty and staff mentor students in inner-city schools. *Middle School Journal, 25* (1), 65-67.

Fitzpatrick, J. P. (1987). *Puerto Rican Americans* (2nd ed.). Englewood Cliffs, NJ: Prentice-Hall.

Friesen, J. W., & Wieler, E. E. (1988). New robes for an old order: Multicultural education, peace education, cooperative learning, and progressive education. *The Journal of Educational Thought, 22(1),* 46-56.

Garcia, R. L. (1984). Countering classroom discrimination. *Theory into Practice, 23,* 104-109.

Garfield, S. (1993). Fostering cross-cultural understanding. *Teaching K-8, 23* (7), 45-47.

Gay, G. (1983). Multiethnic education: Historical developments and future possibilities. *Phi Delta Kappan, 64,* 560-563.

Gay, G. (1992). Effective teaching practices for multicultural classrooms. In C. F. Diaz (Ed.), *Multicultural education for the 21st century* (pp. 38-56). Washington: National Education Association.

Glazer N., & Moynihan, D. P. (1970). *Beyond the melting pot: The Negroes, Puerto Ricans, Jews, Italians, and Irish of New York City* (2nd ed.). Cambridge, MA: The M.I.T. Press.

George, P. S. (1993). Tracking and ability grouping in the middle school: Ten tentative truths. *Middle School Journal, 24* (4), 17-24.

George, P. S., & Alexander, W. M. (1993). *The exemplary middle school* (2nd ed.). New York: Harcourt Brace Jovanovich.

Gollnick, D. M., & Chinn, P. C. (1990). *Multicultural education in a pluralistic society* (3rd ed.). Columbus, OH: Merrill.

Gordon, M. M. (1964). *Human nature, class, and ethnicity.* New York: Oxford University.

Grant, C. A. (1989). Urban teachers: Their new colleagues and curriculum. *Phi Delta Kappan, 70,* 764-770.

Grant, C. A., & Sleeter, C. (1989). *Turning on learning: Five approaches for multicultural teaching plans for race, class, gender, and disability.* Columbus, OH: Merrill.

Green, J. W. (1982). *Cultural awareness in the human services.* Englewood Cliffs, NJ: Prentice-Hall.

Haberman, M. (1991). The pedagogy of poverty versus good teaching. *Phi Delta Kappan, 73,* 290-294.

Hale-Benson, J. E. (1986). *Black children: Their roots and their culture* (rev. ed.). Baltimore, MD: Johns Hopkins.

Hall, E. T. (1981). *Beyond culture.* Garden City, NY: Anchor.

Haring, N. G. (1990). Overview of special education. In N. G. Haring, & L. McCormick (Eds.), *Exceptional children and youth* (pp. 1-45). Columbus, OH: Merrill.

Hartman, J. S., & Askounis, A. C. (1989). Asian-American students: Are they really a "model minority"? *The School Counselor, 37,* 109-111.

Havighurst, R. J. (1972). *Developmental tasks and education.* New York: McKay.

Hepburn, M. A. (1993). Concepts of pluralism and the implications for citizenship education. *Social Studies, 84(1),* 20-26.

Hernandez, H. (1989). *Multicultural education: A teacher's guide to content and process.* Columbus, OH: Merrill.

Hodgkinson, H. (1985). *All one system: The demographics of education.* Washington: Educational Leadership Institute.

Irwin, J. L. (Ed.). (1992). *Transforming middle level education.* Boston: Allyn and Bacon.

James, M. (1986). *Advisor-advisee programs: Why, what, and how.* Columbus, OH: National Middle School Association.

Johnston, J. H. (1992). Youth as cultural and economic capital: Learning how to be. In J.L. Irwin (Ed.) *Transforming middle level education,* (pp. 46-62). Boston: Allyn and Bacon.

Kitano, H. H. L. (1989). A model for counseling Asian-Americans. In P. B. Pedersen, J. G. Draguns, W. J. Lonner, & J. E. Trimble (Eds.), *Counseling across cultures,* (pp. 139-151). Honolulu: University of Hawaii Press.

Koff, E., Rierdan, J., & Stubbs, M. L. (1990). Gender, body iamge, and self-concept in early adolescence. *Journal of Early Adolescence, 10,* 56-58.

Larkin, J. M. (1993). Rethinking basic skills instruction with urban students. *The Educational Forum, 57,* 413-419.

Lewis, A. C. (1991). *Gaining ground: The highs and lows of urban middle school reform 1989-1991.* New York: The Edna McConnell Clark Foundation.

Lightfoot, S. L. (1978). *Worlds apart: Relationships between families and schools.* New York: Basic.

Lipsitz, J. (1984). *Successful schools for young adolescents.* New Brunswick, NJ: Transaction Books.

Little Soldier, L. (1989). Cooperative learning and the Native-American student. *Phi Delta Kappan, 71,* 161-163.

Lonner, W. J., & Ibrahim, F. A. (1989). Assessment in cross-cultural counseling. In P. B. Pedersen, J. G. Draguns, J. Lonner, & J. E. Trimble (Eds.), *Counseling across cultures* (3rd ed.). (pp. 299-333). Honolulu: University of Hawaii Press.

Lounsbury, J. H. (1991). A fresh start for the middle school curriculum. *Middle School Journal, 23* (2), 3-7

Lounsbury, J. H. (1993). The challenge of restructuring middle level education. *Contemporary Education, 64* (2), 132-136.

Lounsbury, J. H., & Vars, G. F. (1978). *A curriculum for the middle school years.* New York: Harper & Row.

Lum, D. (1986). *Social work practice and people of color: A process-stage approach.* Monterey, CA: Brooks/Cole.

McCormick, T. (1984). Multiculturalism: Some principles and issues. *Theory into practice, 23,* 93-97.

McEwin, C. K., & Thomason, J. (1991). Curriculum: The next frontier. *Momentum, 22*(2), 34-37.

Mackey, B. J. (1990). Cross-age tutoring: Students teaching students. *Middle School Journal, 22*(1), 24-26.

Madhere, S. (1991). Self-esteem of African-American preadolescents: Theoretical and practical considerations. *Journal of Negro Education, 60,* 47-61.

Maeroff, G. I. (1988). Withered hopes, stillborn dreams: The dismal panorama of urban schools. *Phi Delta Kappan, 70,* 633-638.

Manning, M. L. (1989). Multicultural education. *Middle School Journal, 21*(1), 14-16.

Manning, M. L. (1991). More than lipservice to multicultural education. *The Clearing House, 64,* 218.

Manning, M. L. (1993a). Making equal access a middle school priority. *ACEI Focus on Later Childhood/Early Adolescence, 5*(4), 1-2.

Manning, M. L. (1993b). Cultural and gender differences in young adolescents. *Middle School Journal, 25* (1), 13-17.

Manning, M. L., & Allen, M. G. (1987). Social development in early adolescence: Implications for middle school educators. *Childhood Education, 63,* 172-176.

Manning, M. L., & Baruth, L. G. (1991). Appreciating cultural diversity in the class-room. *Kappa Delta Pi Record, 27*(4), 104-107.

Manning, M. L., & Lucking, R. (1993). Cooperative learning and multicultural classooms. *The Clearing House, 68,* 12-16.

Manning, M. L., & Lucking, R. (1990). Ability grouping: Realities and alternatives. *Childhood Education, 66,* 254-258.

Marion, R. (1979). Minority parent involvement in the IEP process: A systematic model approach. *Teaching Exceptional Children 10*(4), 1-15.

Maryland Department of Education. (1989). *What matters in the middle grades.* Baltimore: Author.

May, S. A. (1993). Redeeming multicultural education. *Language Arts 70,* 364-372.

Miller, S. K. (1992). Changing conceptions of good schools: Implications for reforming urban education. *Education and Urban Society, 25*(1), 71-84.

Miller-Lachman, L. (1992). *Our family, our friends, our world: An annotated guide to significant multicultural books for children and teenagers.* New Providence, NJ: R. R. Bowker.

Mindel, H. C., & Habenstein, R. W. (1981). Family lifestyles of America's ethnic minorities: An introduction. In C. H. Mindel, & R. W. Habenstein (Eds.), *Ethnic families in America: Patterns and variations* (pp. 1-13). New York: Elsevier.

Mirande', A. (1986). Adolescence and Chicano families. In G. K. Leigh, & G. W. Peterson (Eds.), *Adolescents in families* (pp. 433-455). Cincinnati, OH: South-Western.

More, A. J. (1987). Native-American learning styles: A review for researchers and teachers. *Journal of American Indian Education, 27* (1), 17-29.

Murray, C. B., & Clark, R. M. (1990). Targets of racism. *The American School Board Journal, 177* (6), 22-24.

National Association of Secondary School Principals. (1993). *Achieving excellence through the middle level curriculum.* Reston, VA: Author.

National Council for Accreditation of Teacher Education. (1986). *Standards, procedures, and policies for accreditation of professional teacher education units.* Washington: Author.

National Middle School Association. (1992). *This we believe.* Columbus, OH: Author.

Nelson, C., & Keith, J. (1990). Comparisons of female and male early adolescent sex role attitude and behavior development. *Adolescence, 25,* 183-204.

Nieto, S. (1992). We speak in many tongues: Language diversity and multicultural education. In C. F. Diaz (Ed.), *Multicultural education for the 21st century* (pp. 112-136). Washington: National Education Association.

Oakes, J. (1987). *Improving inner-city schools: Current directions in urban school reform.* Santa Anna: The Rand Corporation, ED 291 831.

Olsen, L. (1988). Crossing the schoolhouse border: Immigrant children in California. *Phi Delta Kappan, 70,* 211-218.

O'Malley, J. M., & Chamot, A. U. (1990). *Learning strategies in second language acquisition.* Cambridge: Cambridge University Press.

Ornstein, A. C., & Levine, D. U. (1989). Social class, race, and school achievement: Problems and prospects. *Journal of Teacher Education, 40*(5), 17-23.

Osako, M. M., & Liu, W. T. (1986). Intergenerational relations and the aged among Japanese-Americans. *Research on Aging, 8,* 128-155.

Pang, V. O., Mizokawa, D. T., Morsihima, J. K., Olstad, R. G. (1985). Self-concepts of Japanese-American children. *Journal of Cross-Cultural Psychology, 16,* 99-109.

Pedersen, P. B. (1988). *A handbook for developing multicultural awareness.* Alexandria, VA: American Association of Counseling and Development.

Perez, S. A. (1979). How to effectively teach Spanish-speaking children, even if you're not bilingual. *Language Arts, 56,* 159-162.

Perrone, V. (1991). On standardized testing. *Childhood Education, 67*(3), 131-142.

Phinney, J. S. (1989). Stages of ethnic identity development in minority group adolescents. *Journal of Early Adolescence, 9,* 34-49.

Phinney, J. S., & Tarver, S. (1988). Ethnic identity search and commitment in black and white eighth graders. *Journal of Early Adolescence, 8,* 265-277.

Pine, G. J., & Hilliard, A. G. (1990). Rx for racism: Imperatives for America's schools. *Phi Delta Kappan, 71,* 593-600.

Pinkney, A. (1975). *Black-Americans.* Englewood Cliffs, NJ: Prentice-Hall.

Ponterotto, J. G. (1991). The nature of prejudice revisited: Implications for counseling intervention. *Journal of Counseling and Development, 70,* 216-224.

Popham, W. J. (1993). Circumventing the high costs of authentic assessment. *Phi Delta Kappan, 74,* 470-473.

Purdom, T. L. (1929). *The value of homogeneous ability grouping.* Baltimore: Warwick & York.

Purkey, W. W., & Novak, J. M. (1984). *Inviting school success* (2nd ed.). Belmont, CA: Wadsworth.

Racial division persists 25 years after King killing. (1993, April 4). *New York Times,* p. 16.

Richardson, E. H. (1981). Cultural and historical perspectives in counseling Indians. In D. W. Sue. *Counseling the culturally different,* (pp. 216-255). New York: John Wiley.

Roberts, L. R., Saragiani, P. A., Petersen, A. C., & Newman, J. L. (1990). Gender differences in the relationship between achievement and self-image during early adolescence. *Journal of Early Adolescence, 10,* 159-175.

Rothenberg, D. (1993). Multicultural education (ERIC/EECE Report). *Middle School Journal, 24*(4), 73-75.

Rothman, E., Schiff, M., Adamyk, M., & Sumegi, Z. (1988). *Multiculturalism in Canada: A public education stratgegy.* ED 330 732.

Sadker M., & Sadker, D. (1982). *Sex equity handbook for schools* (2nd ed.). White Plains, NY: Longman.

Sadker, M., Sadker, D., & Long, L. (1993). Gender and educational equality. In J. A. Banks, & C. A. McGee Banks (Eds.), *Multicultural education: Issues and perspectives* (2nd ed.) (pp. 111-128). Boston: Allyn and Bacon.

Samuda, R. J., & Lewis, J. (1992). Evaluation practices for the multicultural classroom. In C. F. Diaz (Ed.), *Multicultural education for the 21st century* (pp. 97-111). Washington: National Education Association.

Sanders, D. (1987). Cultural conflicts: An important factor in the academic failures of American Indian students. *Journal of Multicultural Counseling and Development, 15,* 81-90.

Santrock, J. W. (1990). *Life-span development* (3rd ed.). Dubuque, IA: Wm. C. Brown.

Shade, B. (1982). Afro-American cognitive style: A variable in school success? *Review of Educational Research, 52,* 219-244.

Shea, T.M., & Bauer, A.M. (1985). *Parents and teachers of exceptional children: A handbook for involvement.* Boston: Allyn and Bacon.

Skaalvik, E. M. (1990). Gender differences in general academic self-esteem and in success expectations on defined academic problems. *Journal of Educational Psychology, 82,* 593-598.

Slavin, R. E. (1983). *An introduction to cooperative learning.* White Plains, NY: Longman.

Slavin, R. E. (1987). *Cooperative learning* (2nd ed.). Washington, DC: National Education Association.

Slavin, R. E. (1988). Cooperative learning and student achievement. *Educational Leadership, 47*(4), 31-33.

Sleeter, C. E., & Grant, C. A. (1988). *Making choices for multicultural education: Five approaches to race, class, and gender.* Columbus, OH: Merrill.

Smith, E. J. (1981). Cultural and historical perspectives in counseling Blacks. In D. W. Sue, *Counseling the culturally different* (pp. 141-185). New York: John Wiley.

Smith, G. R., & Otero, G. G. (1985). *Teaching about cultural differences: Grades 4-12.* Denver, CO: University of Denver, Center for Teaching International Relations.

Stanford, B. H. (1992). Gender equity in the classroom. In D.A. Brynes, & G. Kiger (Eds.), *Common bonds: Anti-bias teaching in a diverse society* (pp. 87-104). Wheaton, MD: Association for Childhood Education International.

Stavro, S. (1993). Developing intercultural sensitivity in the middle years. *Middle School Journal, 24*(4), 70-72.

Stevenson, C. (1992). *Teaching ten to fourteen year olds.* White Plains, NY: Longman.

Stewart, W. J. (1991). Optimizing learning in the urban school. *American Secondary Education, 19(4),* 12-17.

Stover, D. (1990). The new racism. *The American School Journal, 177(6),* 14-18.

Strubbe, M. (1990). Are interdisciplinary units worthwhile? *Middle School Journal, 21(3),* 36-38.

Sue, D. W., & Sue, S. (1983). Counseling Chinese-Americans. In D.R. Atkinson, G. Morten, & D. W. Sue (Eds.), *Counseling American minorities: A cross-cultural perspective* (2nd ed.). (pp. 97-106). Dubuque, IA: Wm. C. Brown.

Sue, D. W. (1981). *Counseling the culturally different.* New York: John Wiley.

Swisher, K. (1992). Learning styles: Implications for teachers. In C. F. Diaz (Ed.), *Multicultural education for the 21st century* (pp. 72-84). Washington: National Education Association.

Tetreault, M. K. T. (1993). Classrooms for diversity: Rethinking curriculum and pedagogy. In J. A. Banks, & C. A. McGee Banks (Eds.) *Multicultural education: Issues and perspectives* (2nd ed.) (pp.129-148). Boston: Allyn and Bacon.

Thomas, R., & Murr, A. (1993, August 9). The economic cost of immigration. *Newsweek,* pp. 18-19.

Thornburg, H. (1982). The total early adolescent in contemporary society. *The High School Journal, 65,* 272-278.

Tiedt, P. L., & Tiedt, I. M. (1990). Multicultural teaching: *A handbook of activities, information, and resources* (3rd ed.). Boston: Allyn and Bacon.

Tucker, B., & Huerta, C. (1987). A study of developmental tasks as perceived by young adult Mexican-American females. *Lifelong Learning: An Omnibus of Practice and Research,18(4),* 4-7.

Urban eighth graders need help. (1993). *High Strides: The Bimonthly Report on Urban Middle Grades, 5(4),* 2.

U. S. Bureau of the Census. (1986). Current population reports, Series P-25, No. 985. *Estimates of the population of the United States, by age, sex, and race. 1980-1985.* Washington, DC: Author.

U. S. Bureau of the Census. (1988). Current Population Reports, Series P-20, No. 431. Washington, DC: Author.

U. S. Bureau of the Census. (1990, September). *We the ....first Americans.* C 3.2: AM 3/ 19. Washington, DC: Author.

U. S. Bureau of the Census. (1990a). *Asians and Pacific Islanders in the U.S.* C 3.223.10: 1990, CP 3-5. Washington, DC: Author.

U. S. Bureau of the Census. (1990b). *Persons of Hispanic origin in the U.S.* C 3.223.10: 1990, CP-3-3. Washington, DC: Author.

U. S. Bureau of the Census. (1991a). *Statistical abstracts of the United States: 1991* (111th ed.). Washington, DC: Author.

U. S. Bureau of the Census. (1991b). *1990 Census Profile, Race and Hispanic Origin* (no. 2 June, 1991), 1-8. Washington, DC: Author.

U. S. Bureau of the Census. (1992). *Statistical abstracts of the United States: 1992* (112th ed.). Washington, DC: Author.

U. S. Bureau of the Census. (1993a, September). *We the American...Blacks.* C 3.2 AM 3/ 14. Washington, DC: Author.

U. S. Bureau of the Census. (1993b, September). *We the American...Asians.* C 3.2 AM 3/ 13. Washington, DC: Author.

U. S. Bureau of the Census. (1993c, September). *We the American... Pacific Islanders.* C 3.2: AM 3/15. Washington, DC: Author.

U. S. Bureau of the Census. (1993d, November). *We the American...Hispanics.* C 3.2: AM 3/18. Washington, DC: Author.

Valentin, T. (1993). English as a second language: Get ready for the onslaught. *NASSP Bulletin, 76(5),* 30-38.

VanBalkom, W. D. (1991). Multicultural education in Alberta's teacher training institutions. *Education Canada, 31,* 46-48.

Werner, E.E. (1979). *Cross-cultural child development: A view from the planet earth.* Monterey, CA: Brooks/Cole.

West, B. E. (1983). The new arrivals from Southeast Asia: Getting to know them. *Childhood Education, 60,* 84-89.

Wheelock, A. (1993). *Crossing the tracks: How "untracking" can save America's schools.* New York: The New Press.

Yokota, J. (1993). Issues in selecting multicultural children's literature. *Language Arts, 70,* 156-167.